SENIORS COLORING BOOK

BELONGS TO:

_____

_____

_____

We have designed the image on single-slide pages to reduce the bleed-through to the next image.
If you are using markers, is recommended to slide a piece of cardstock or paper behind the page you are working on to make sure the ink doesn't stain the next page.

Relax and happy coloring!

Enjoy the time for yourself!

Test your color here

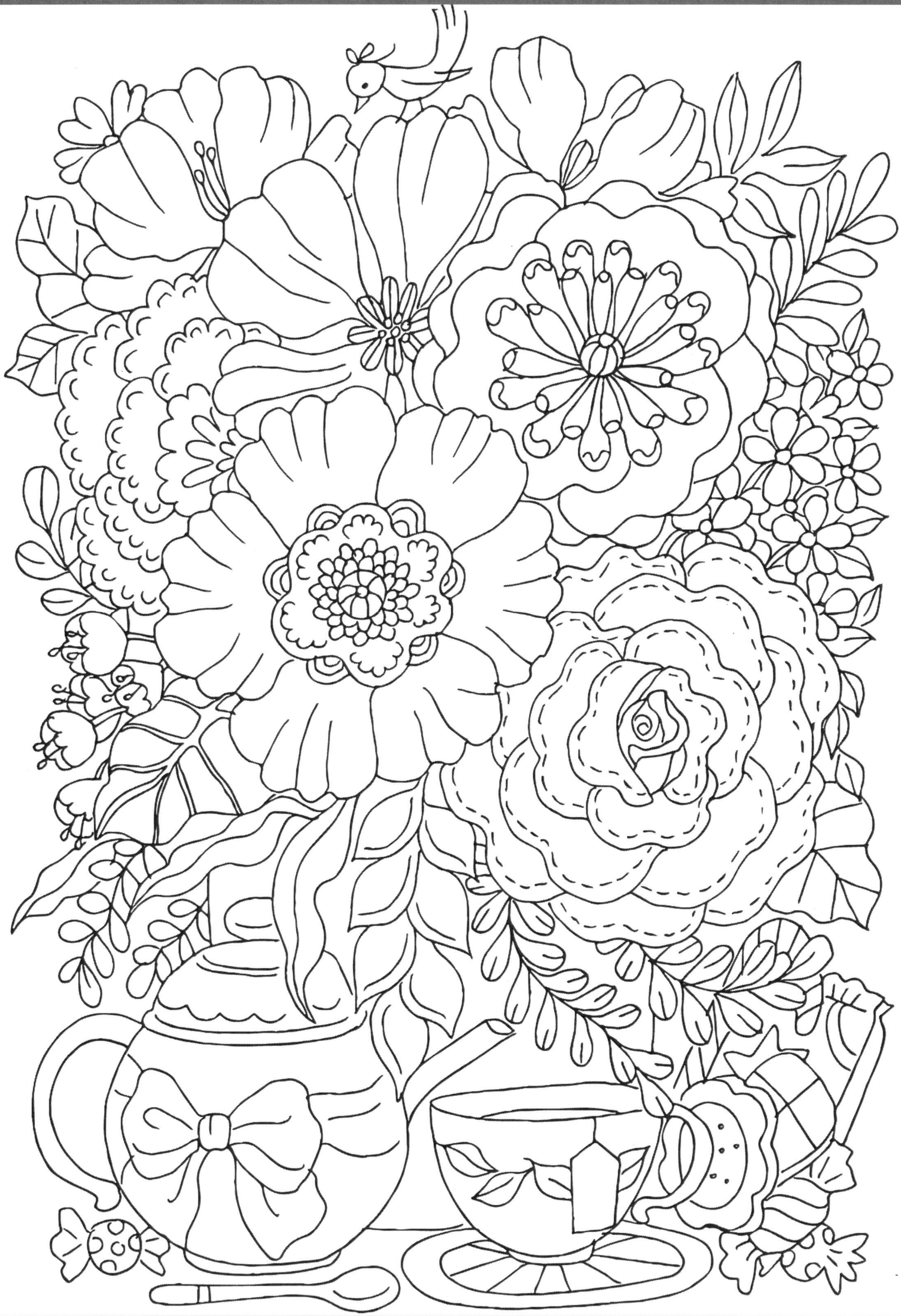

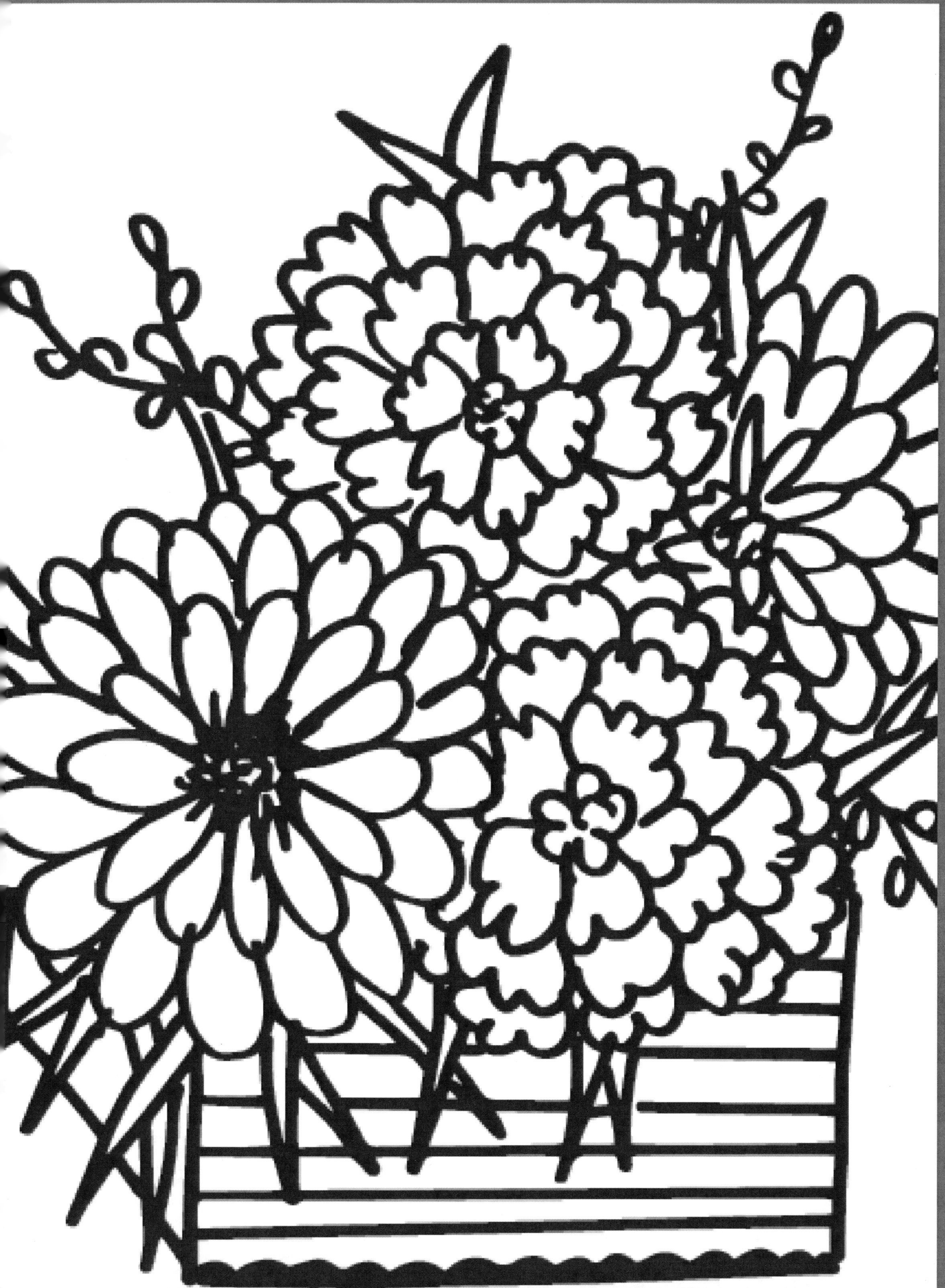

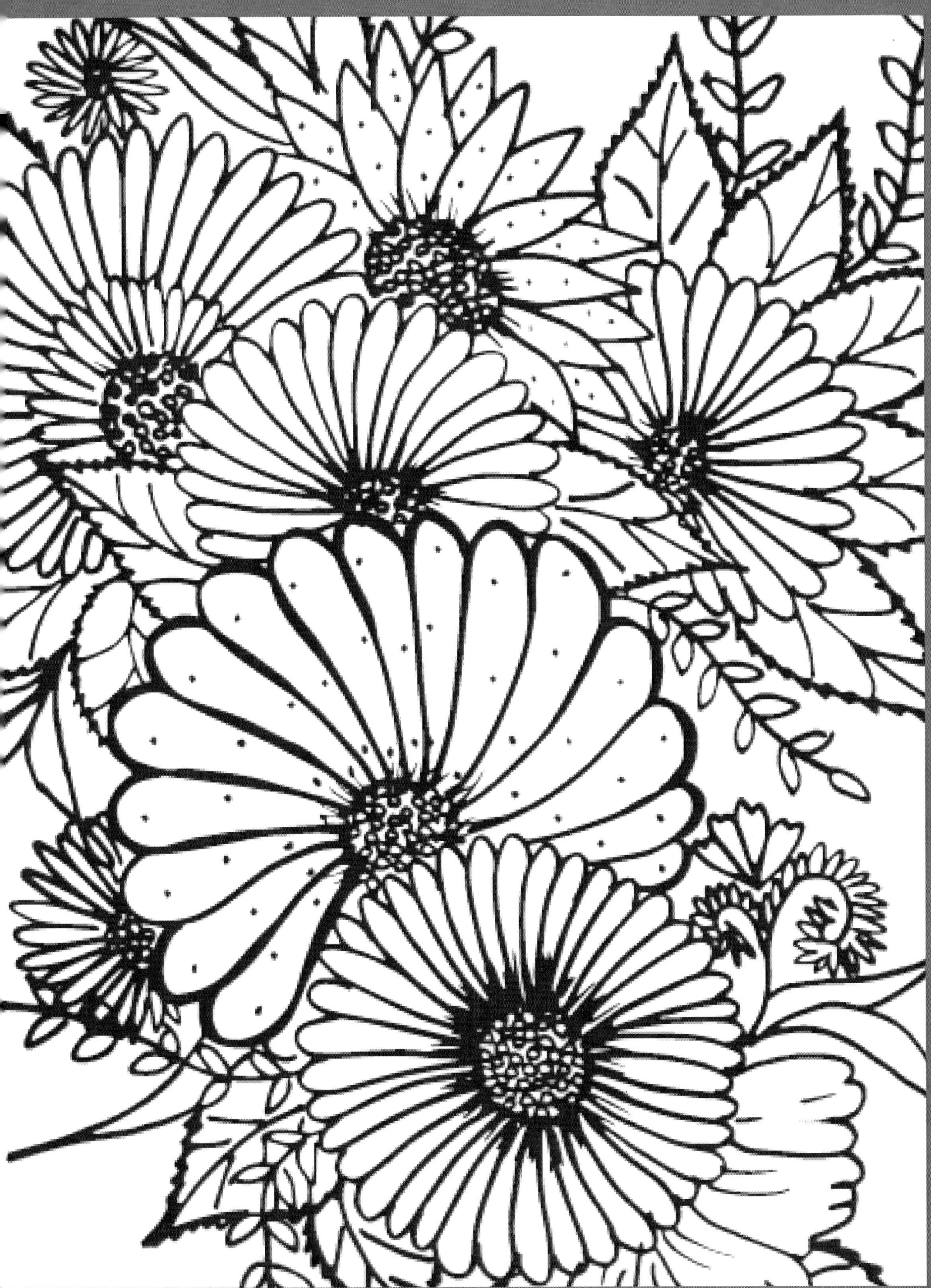

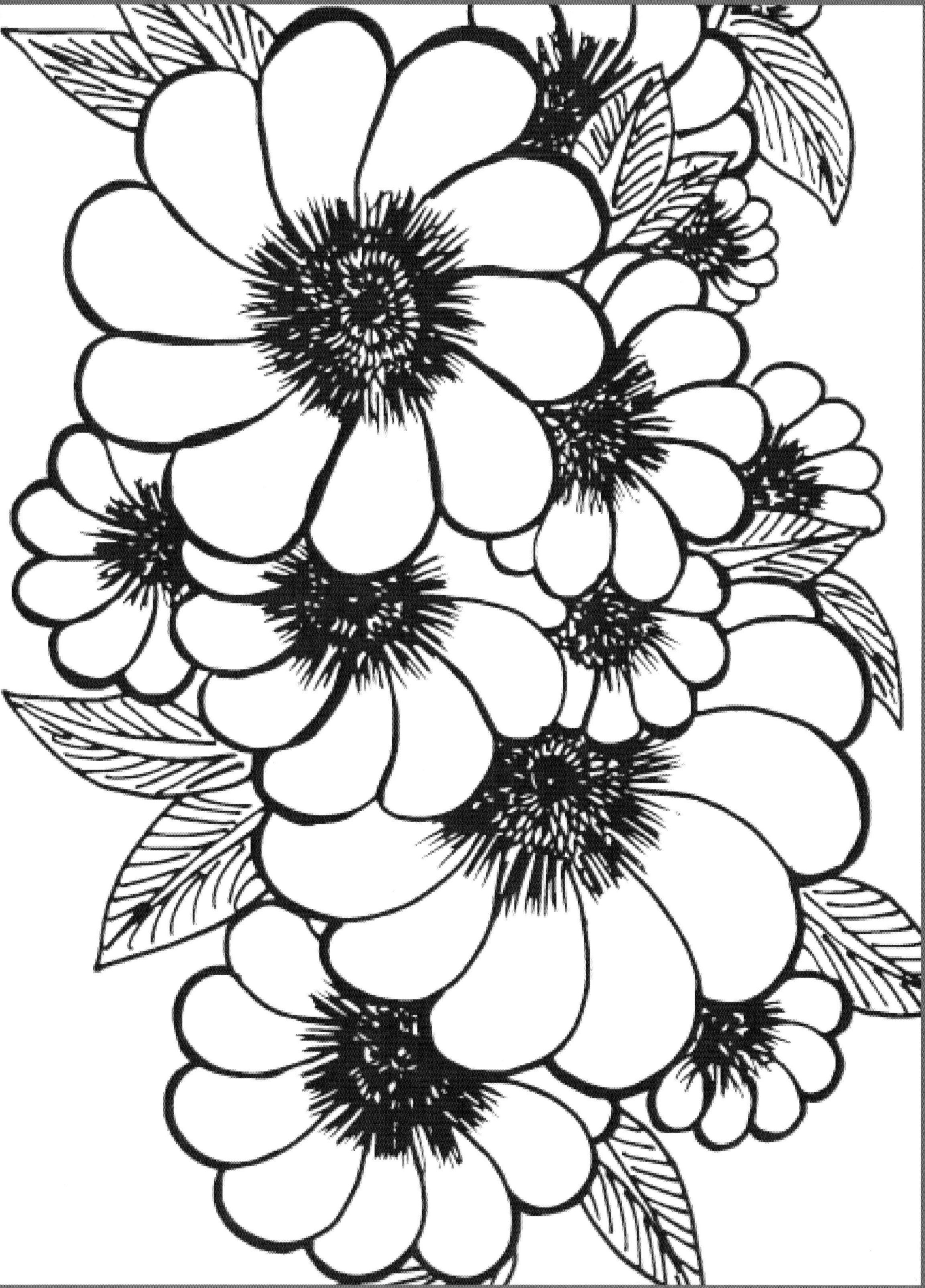

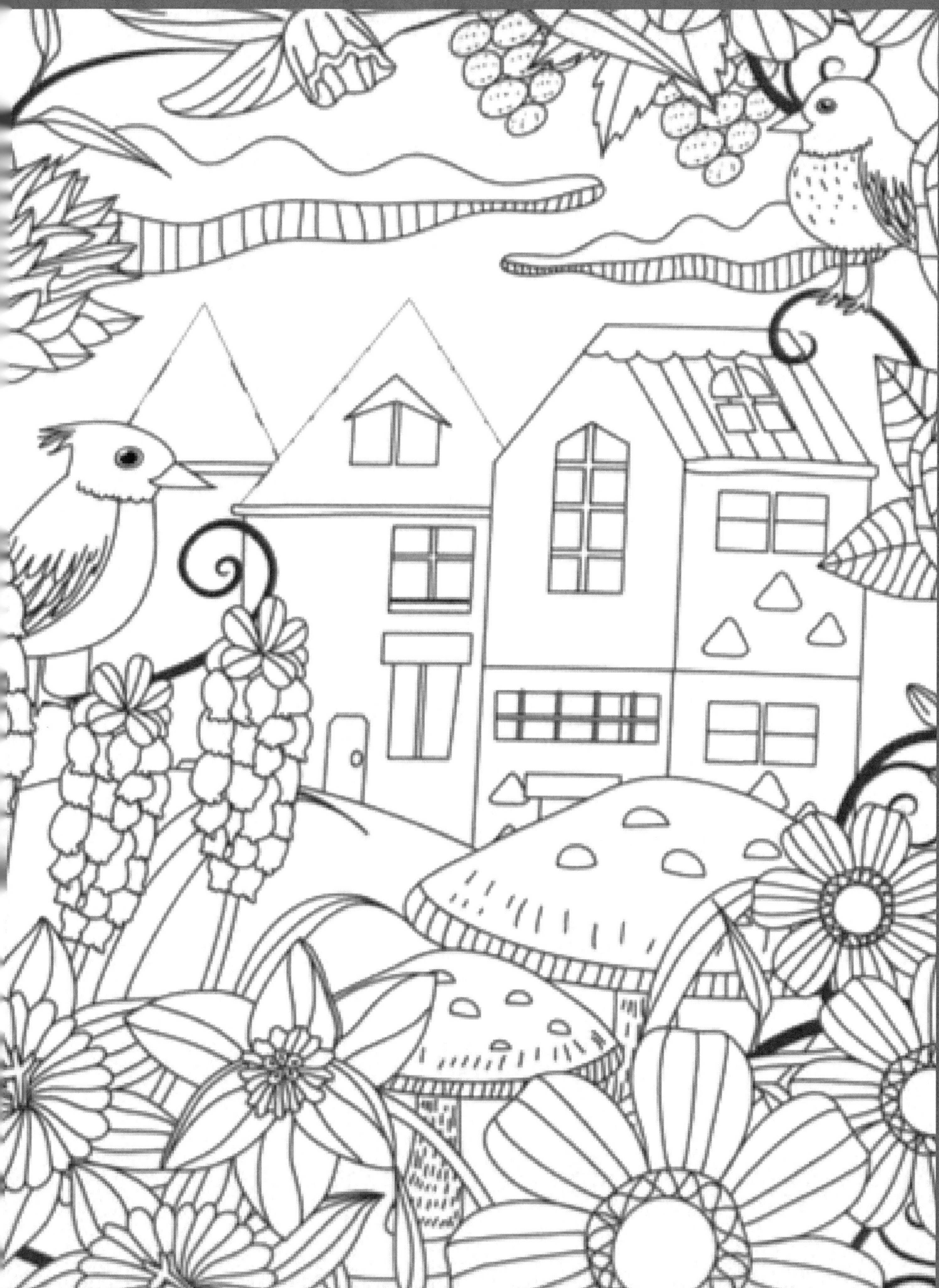

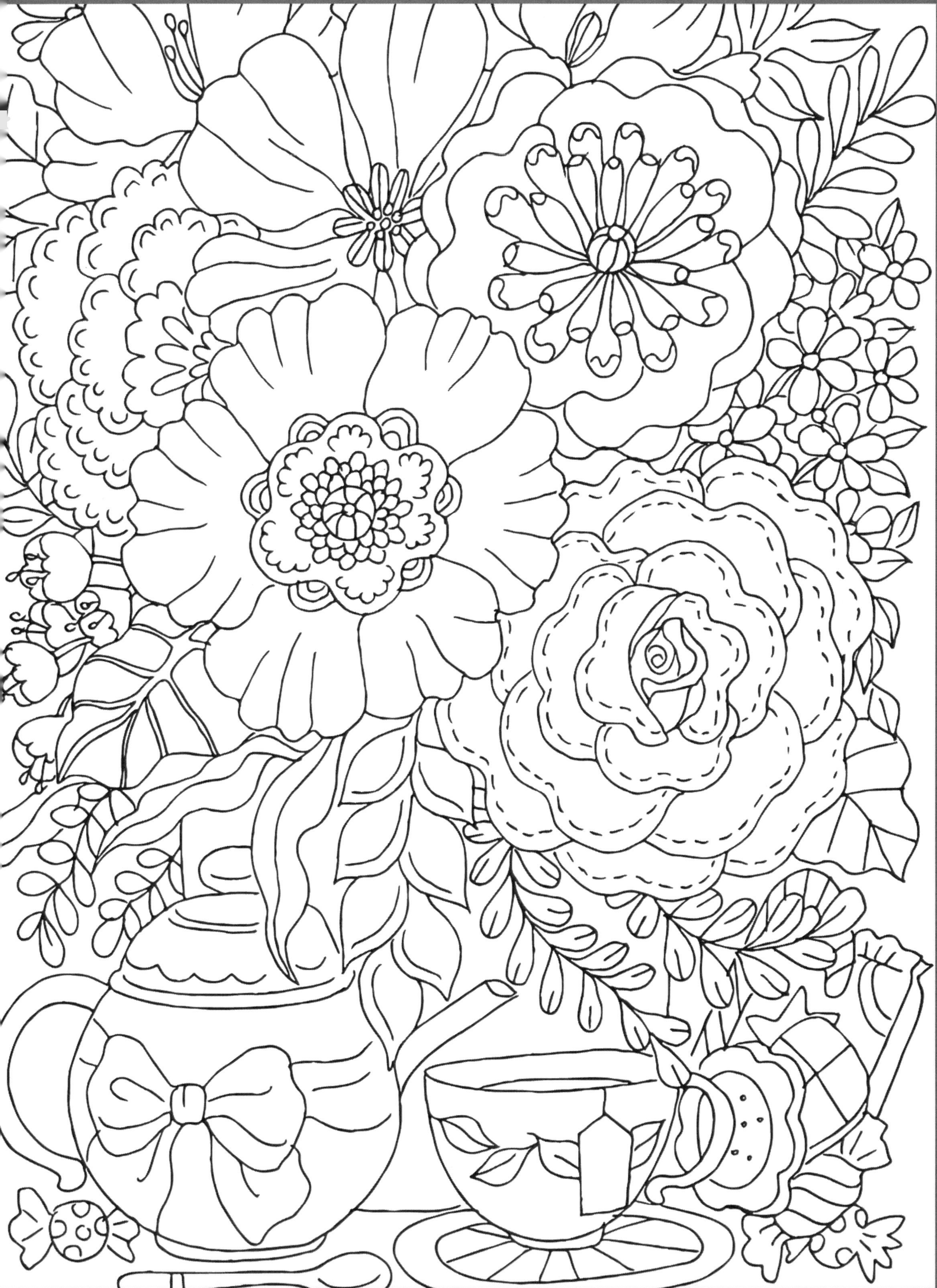

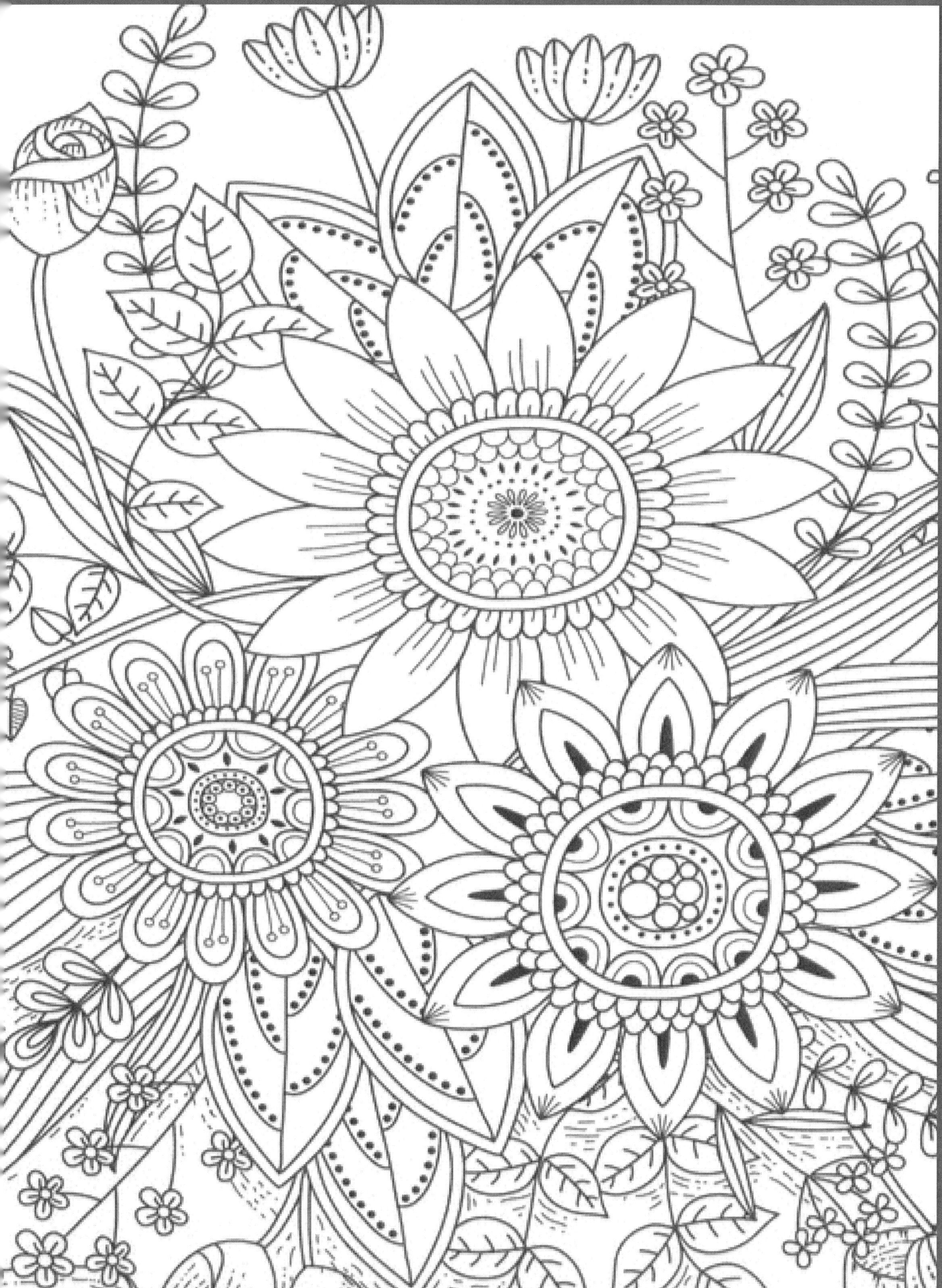

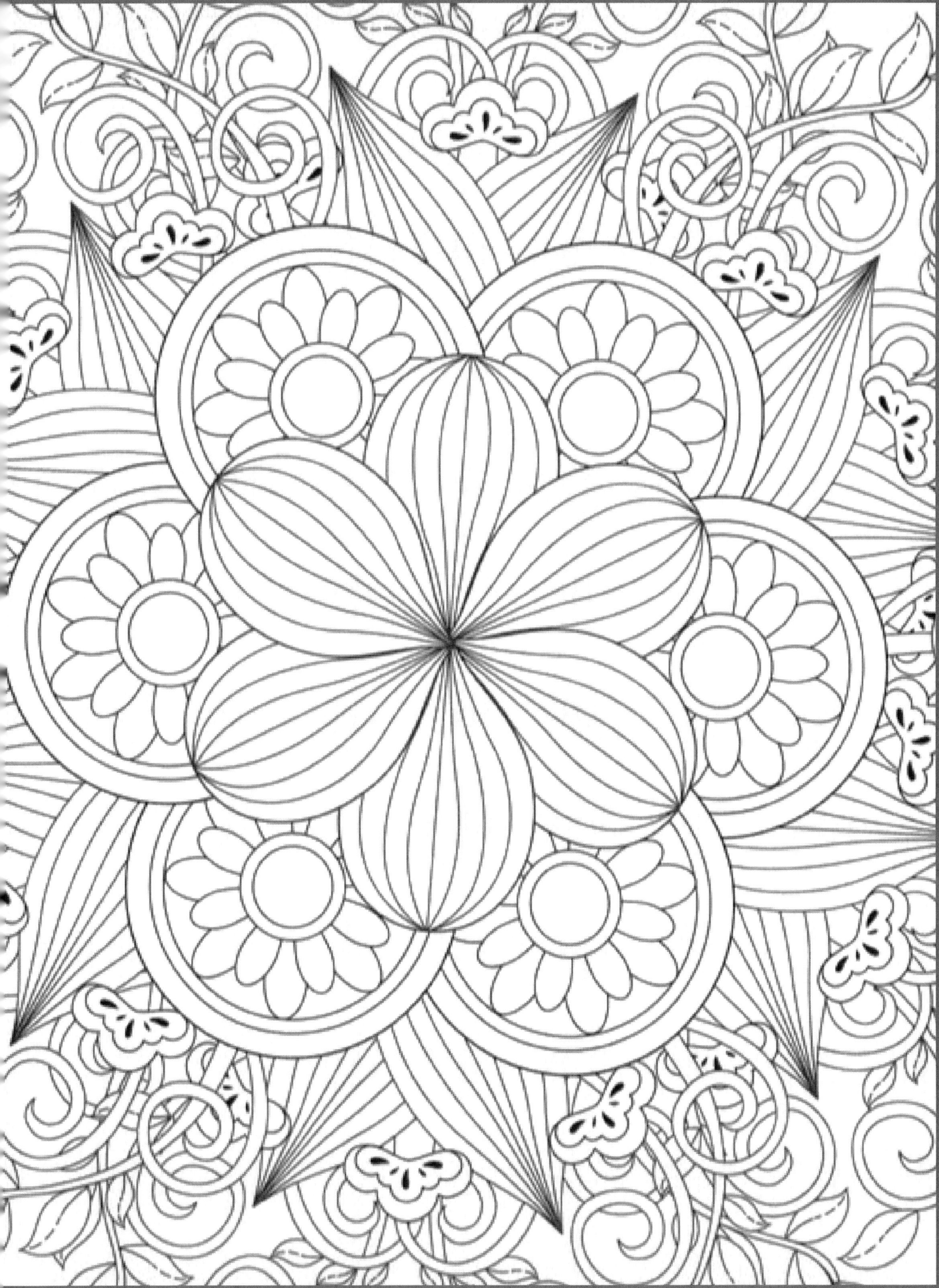

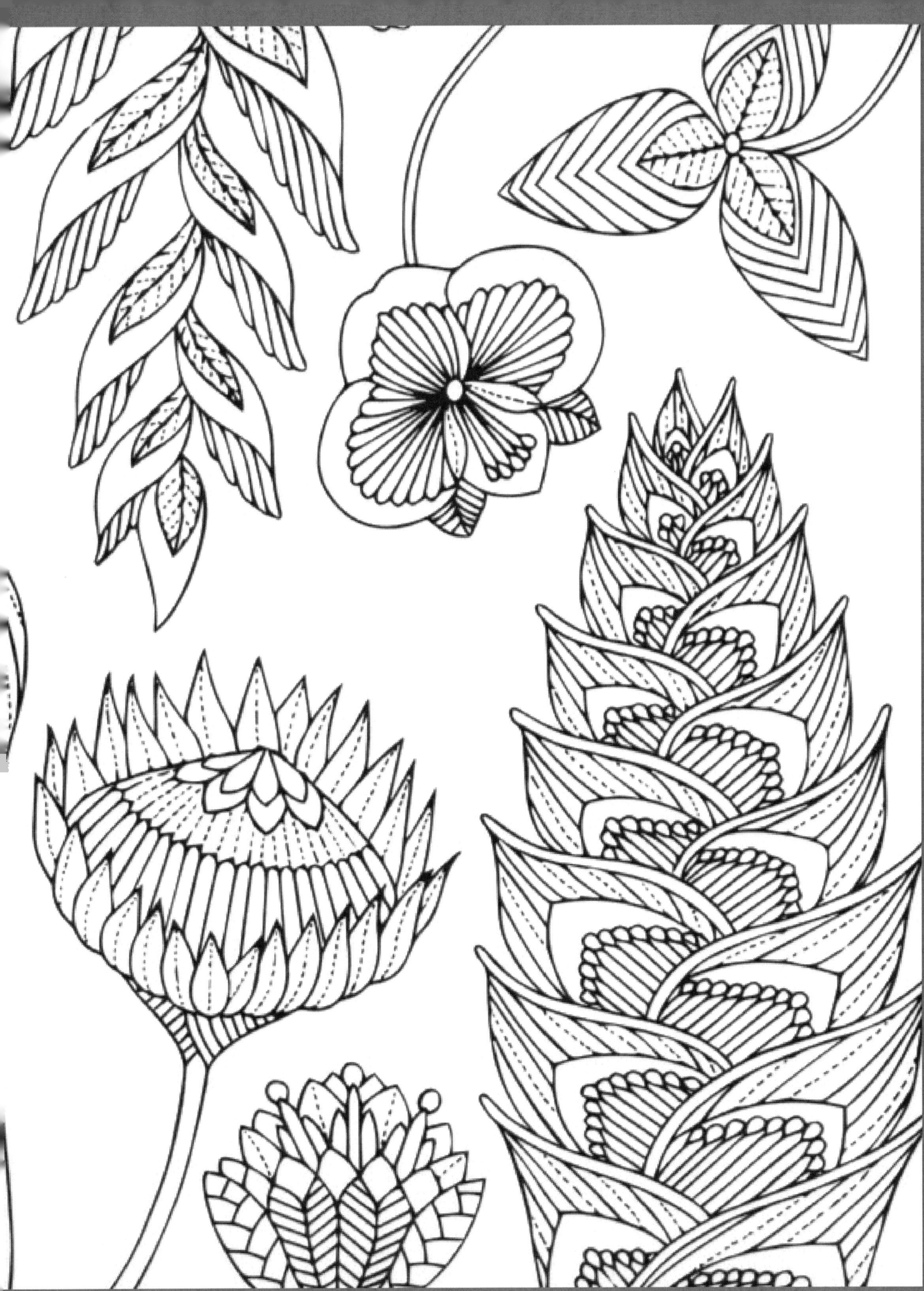

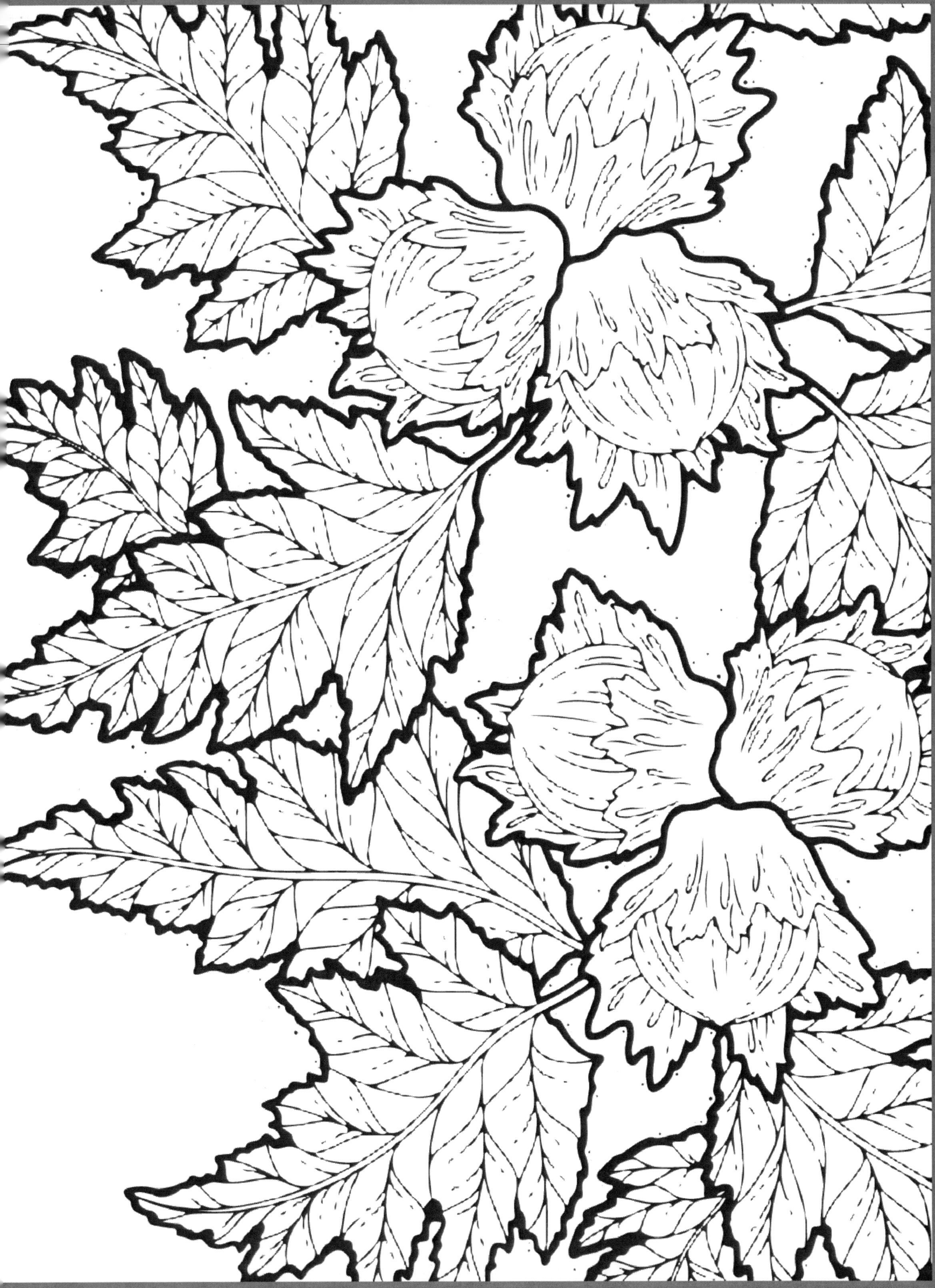

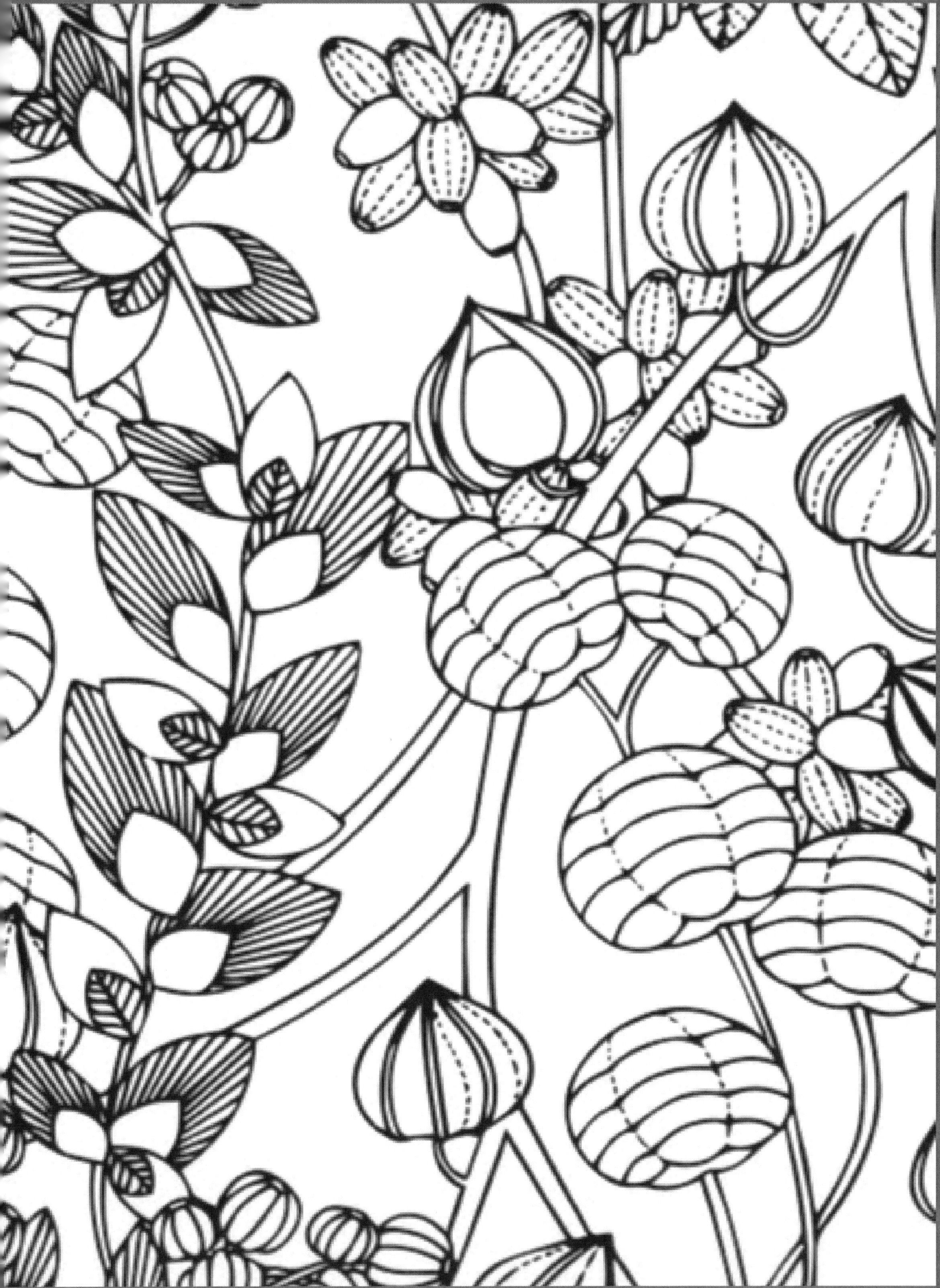

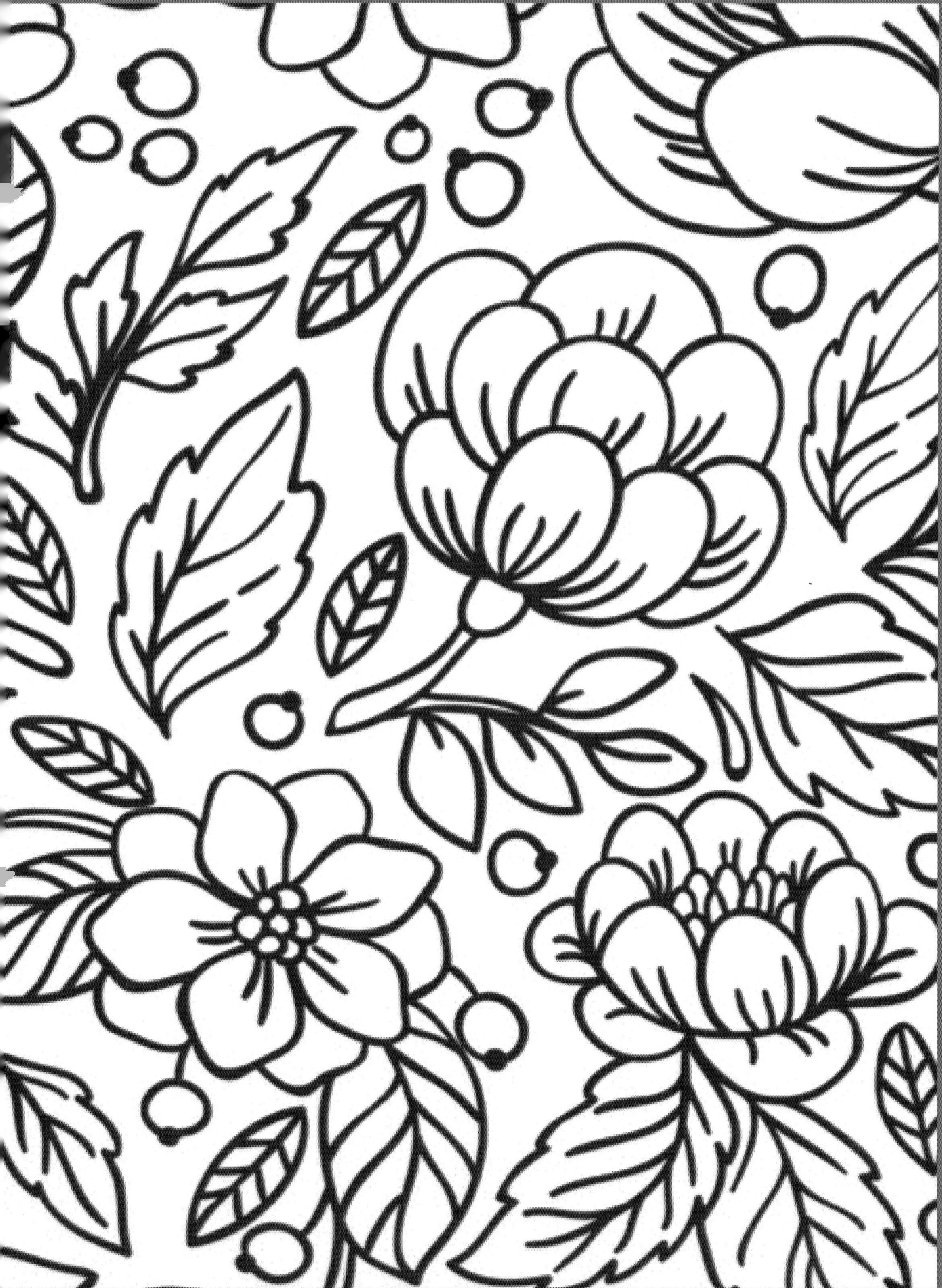

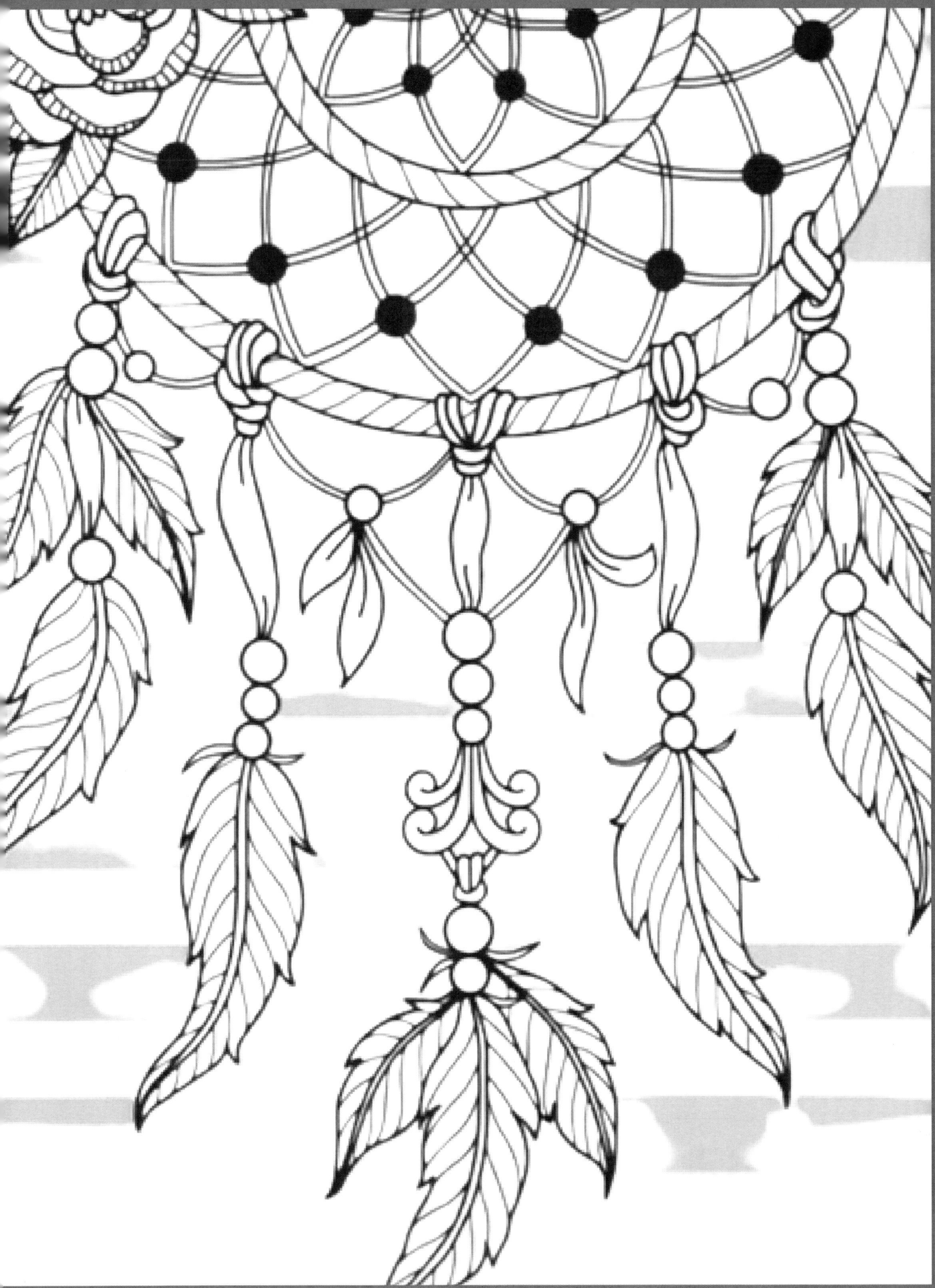

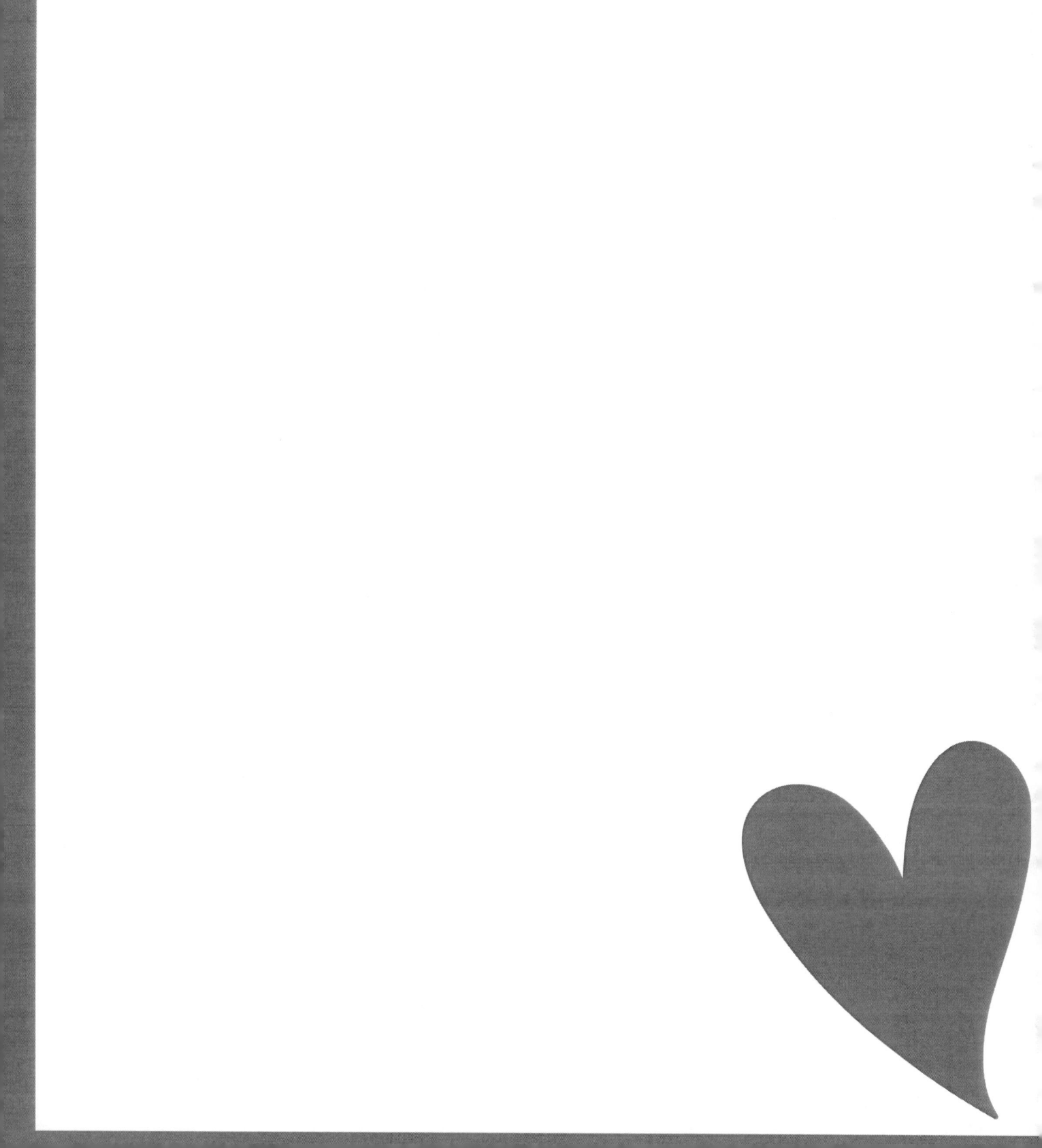

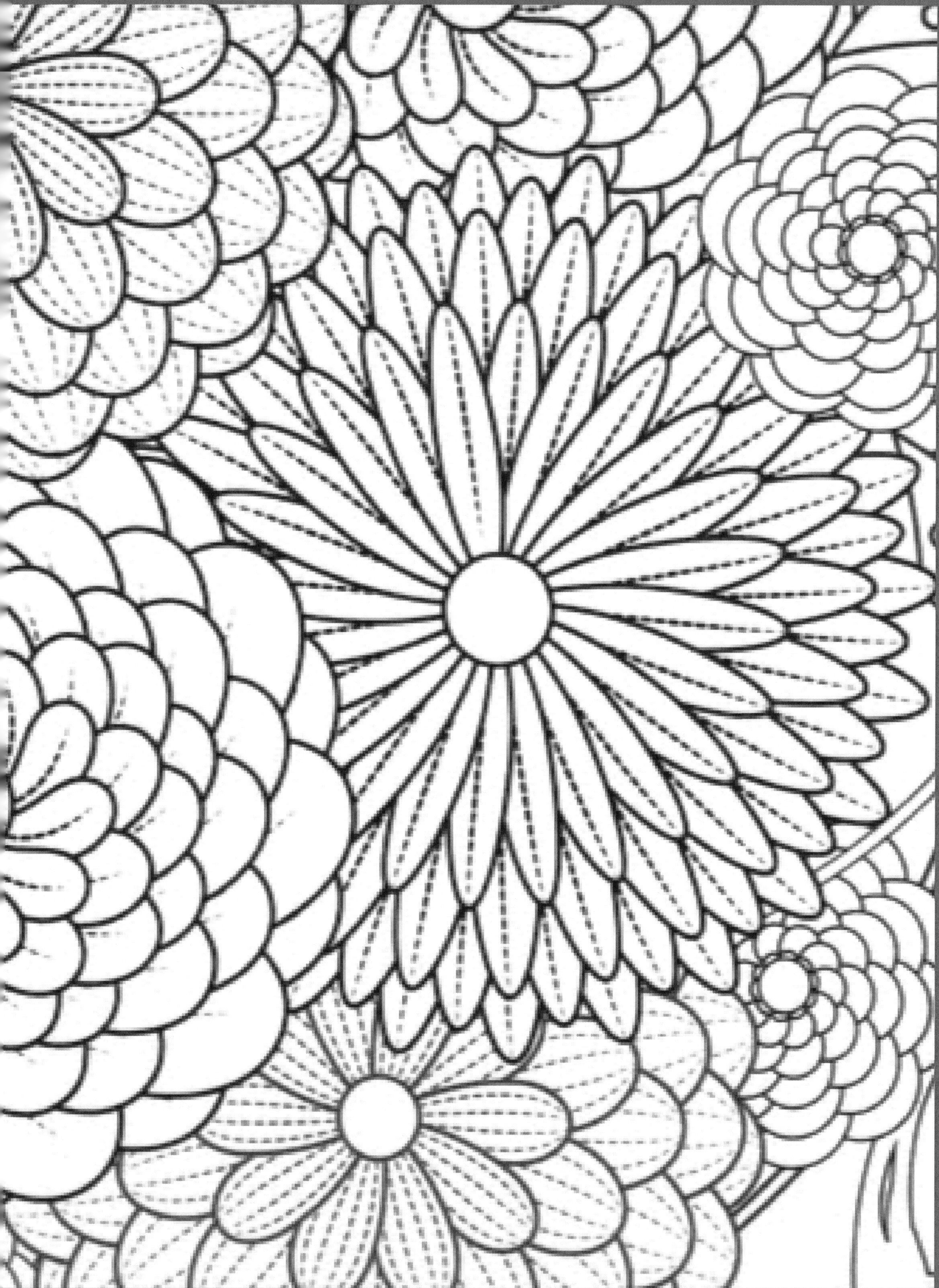

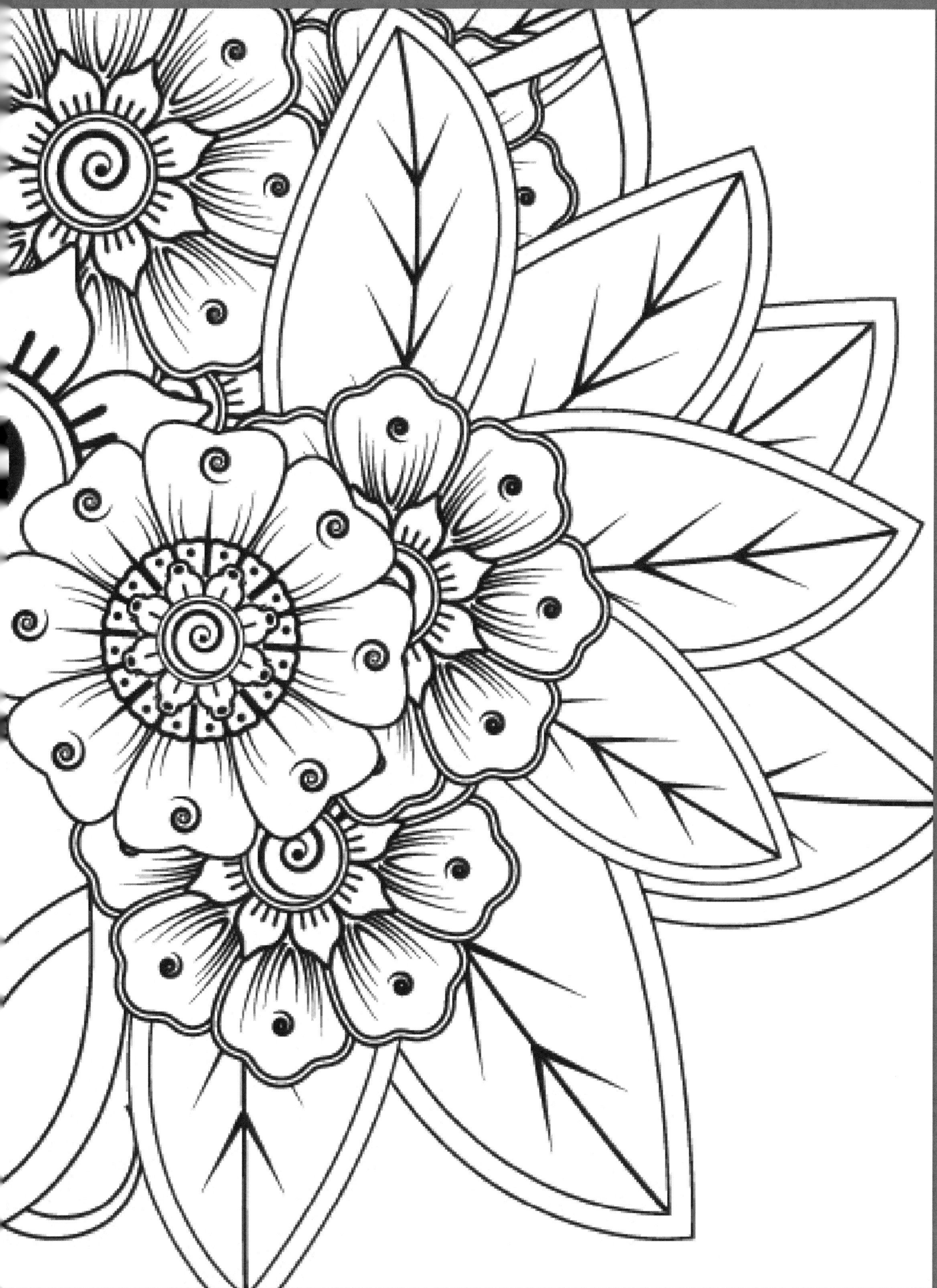

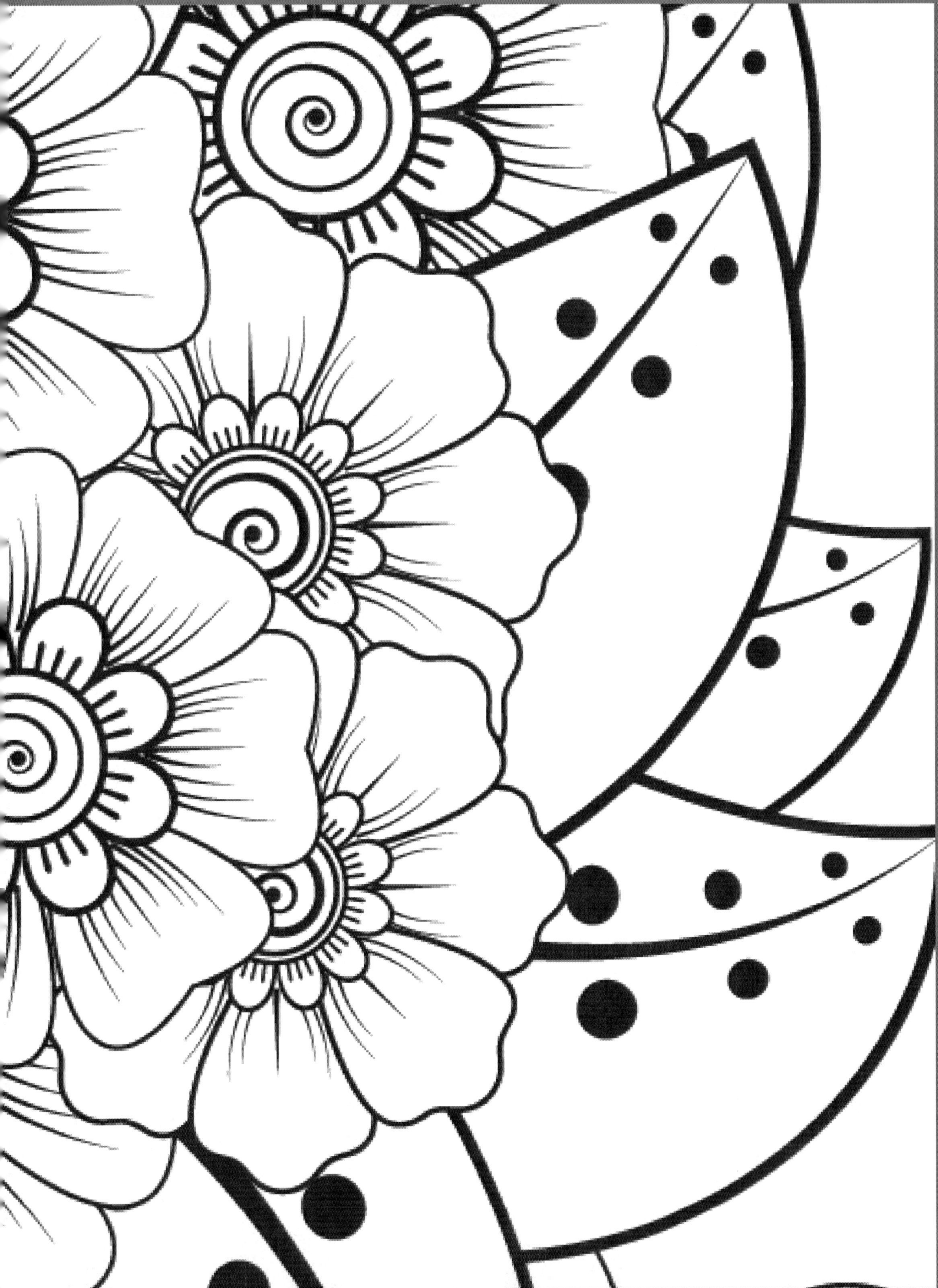

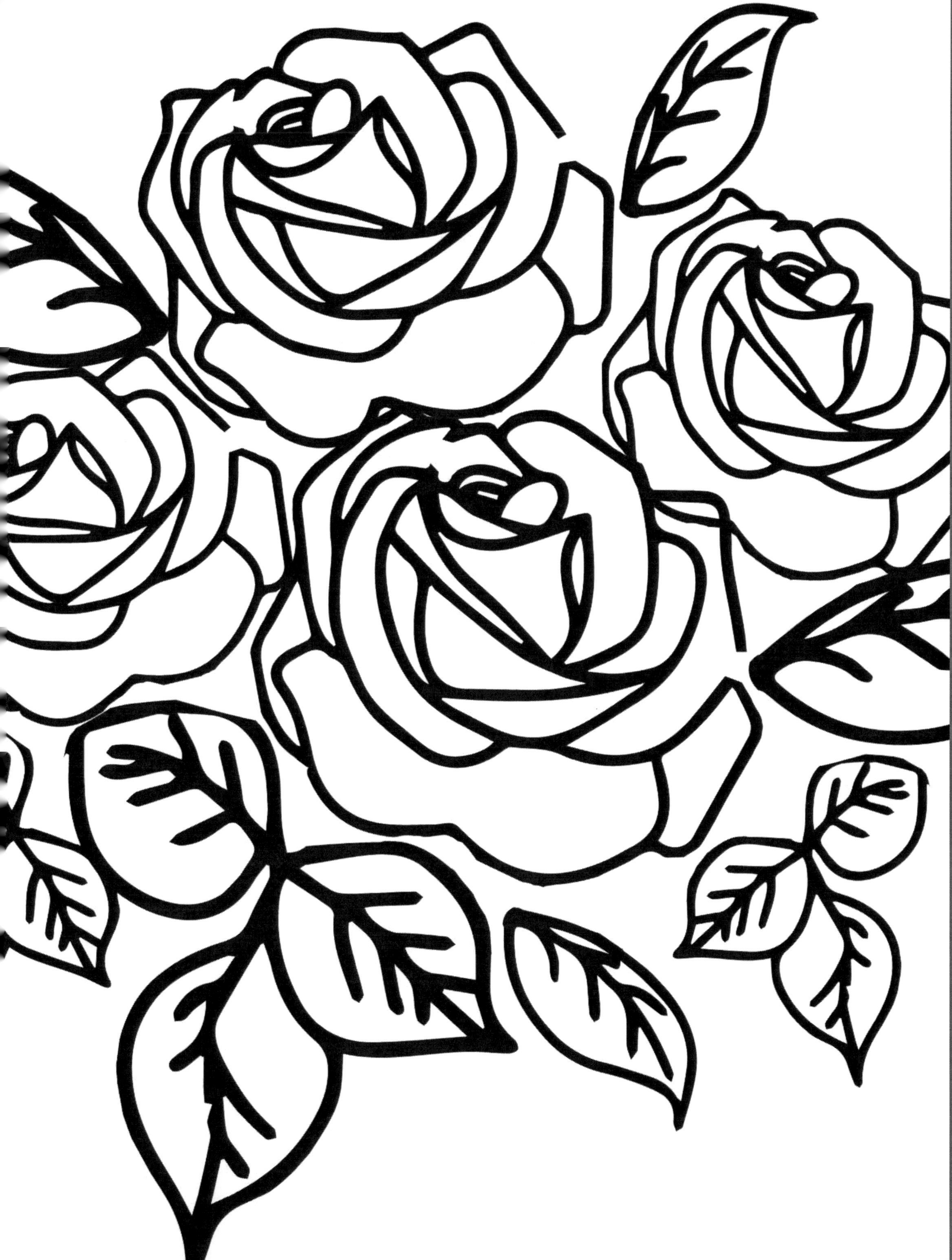

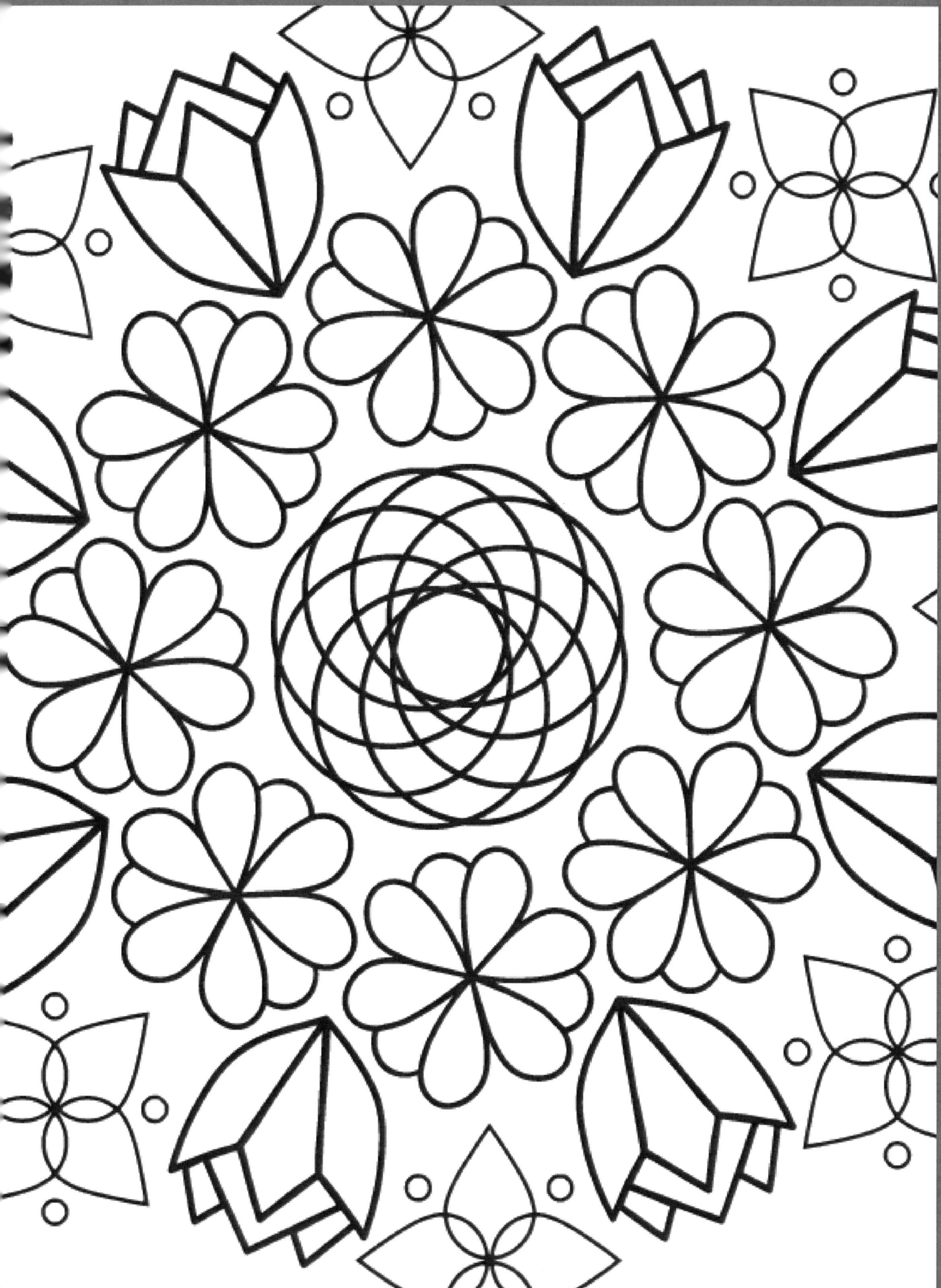

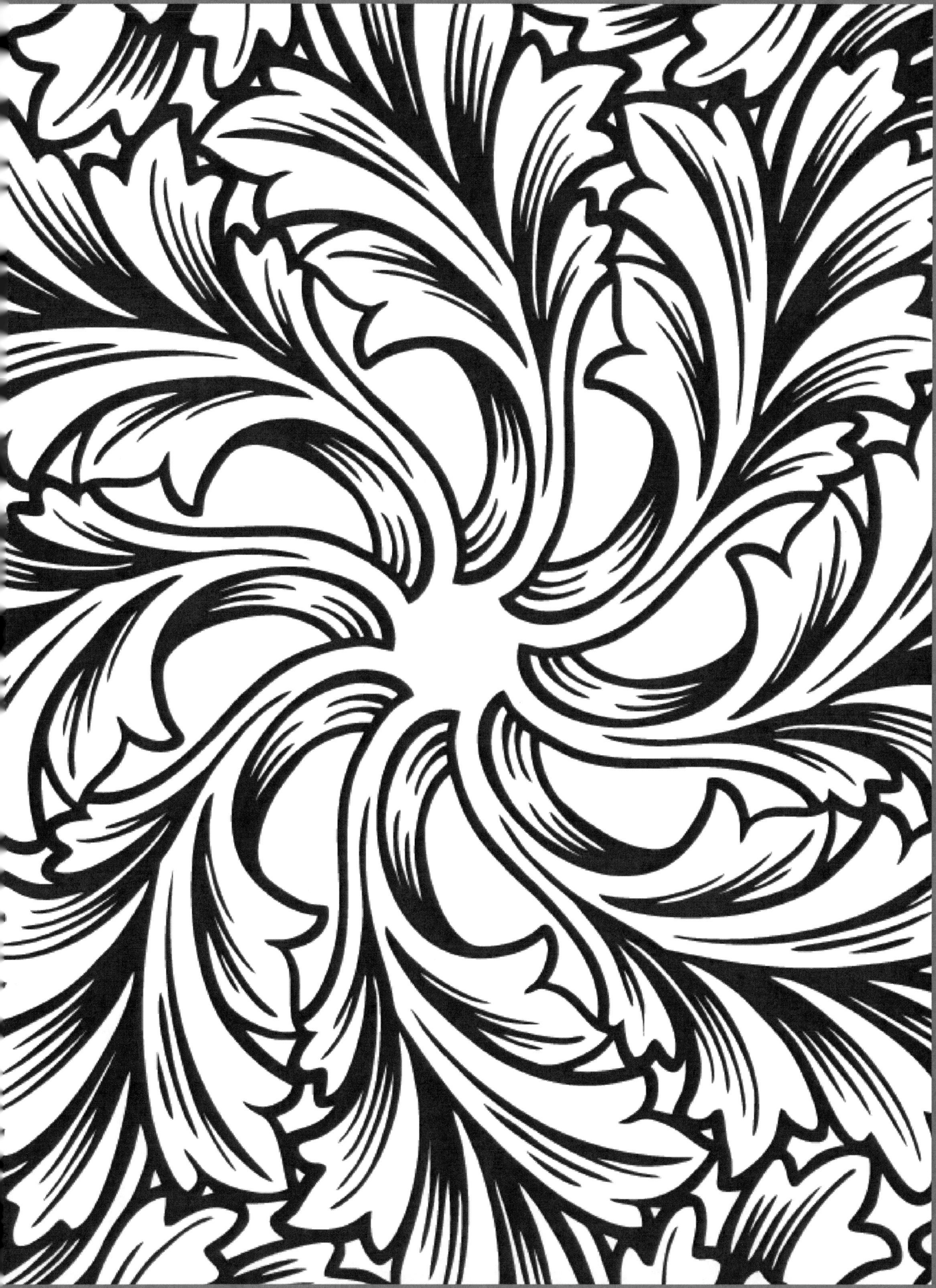

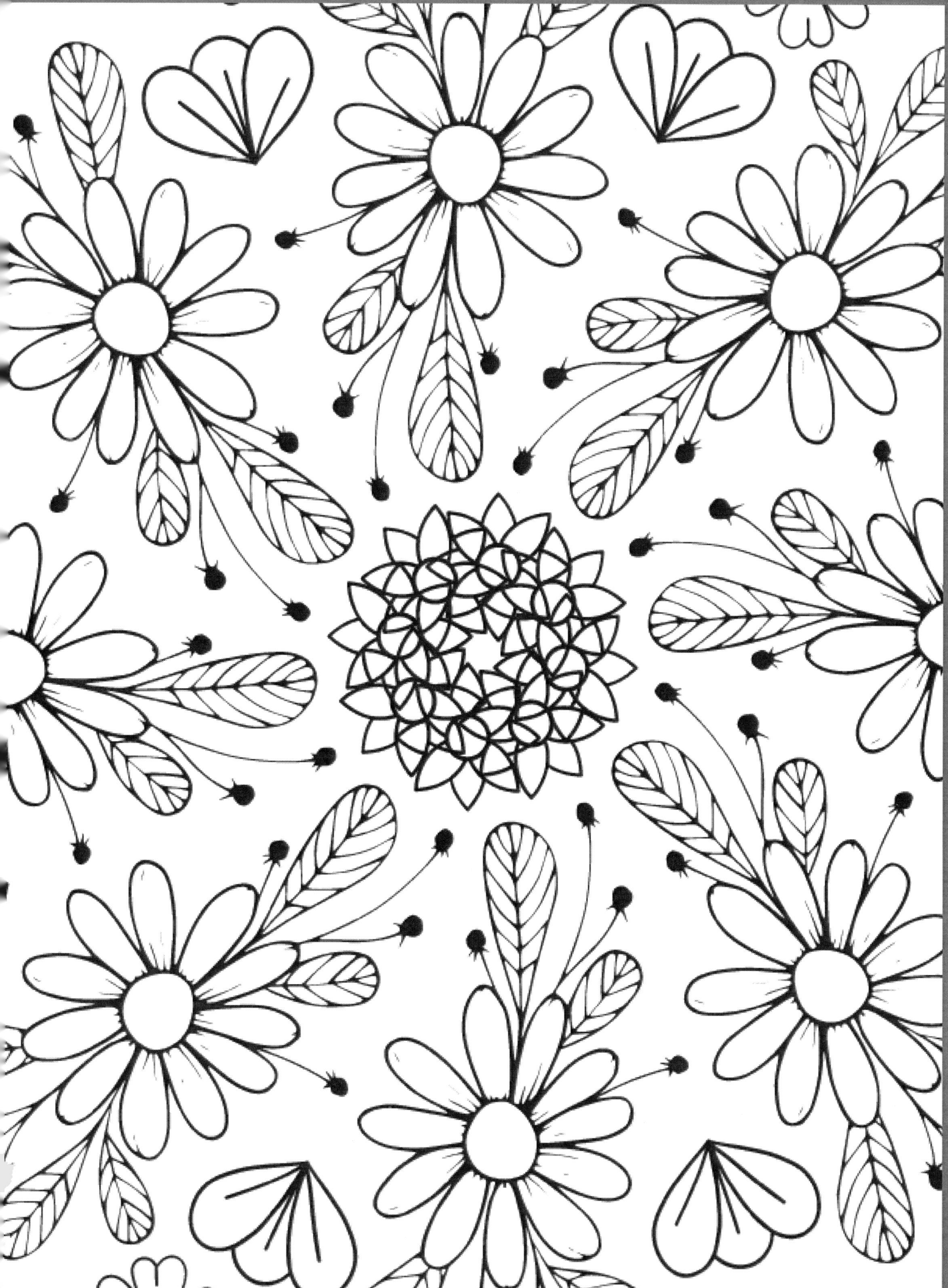

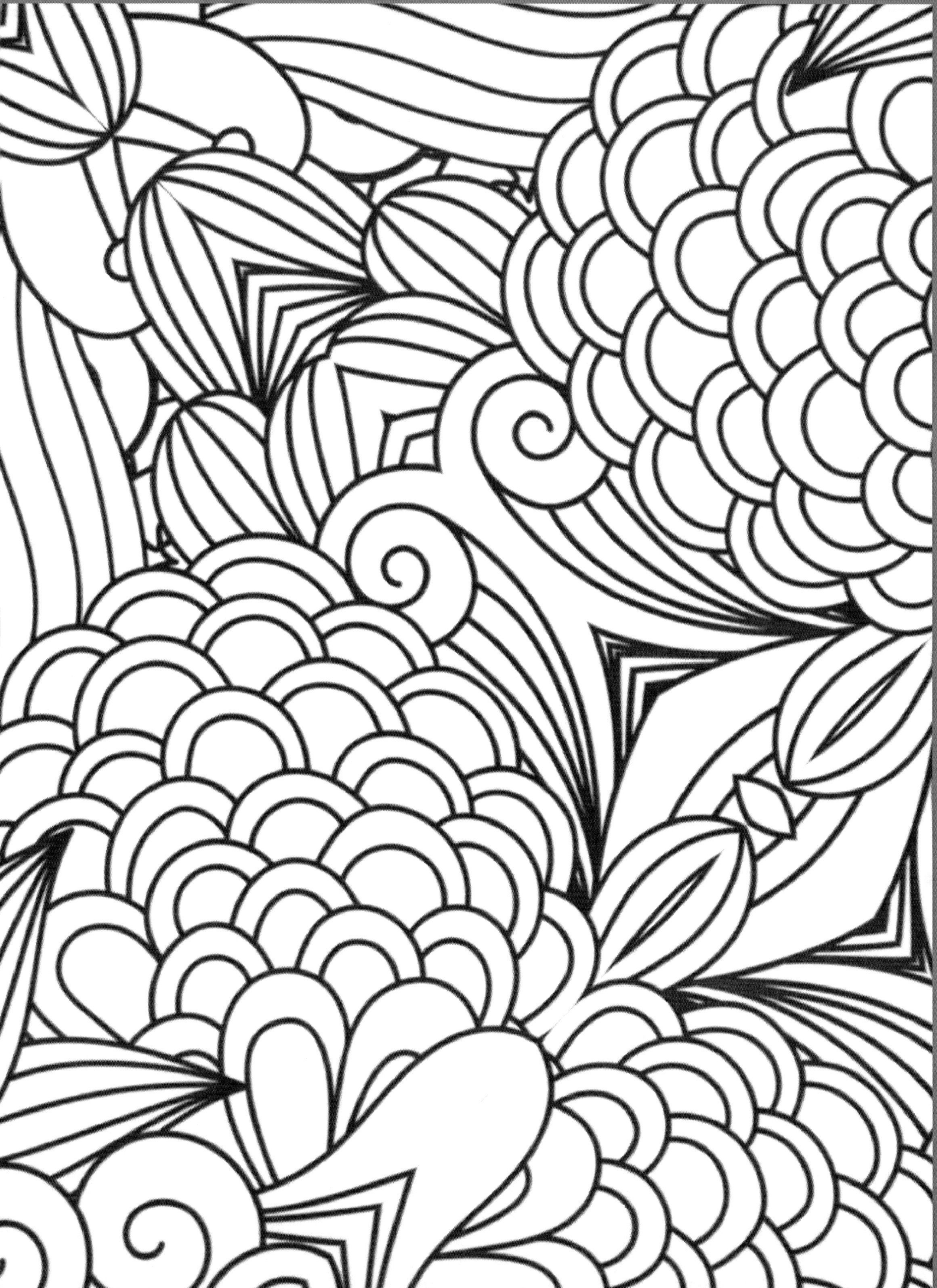

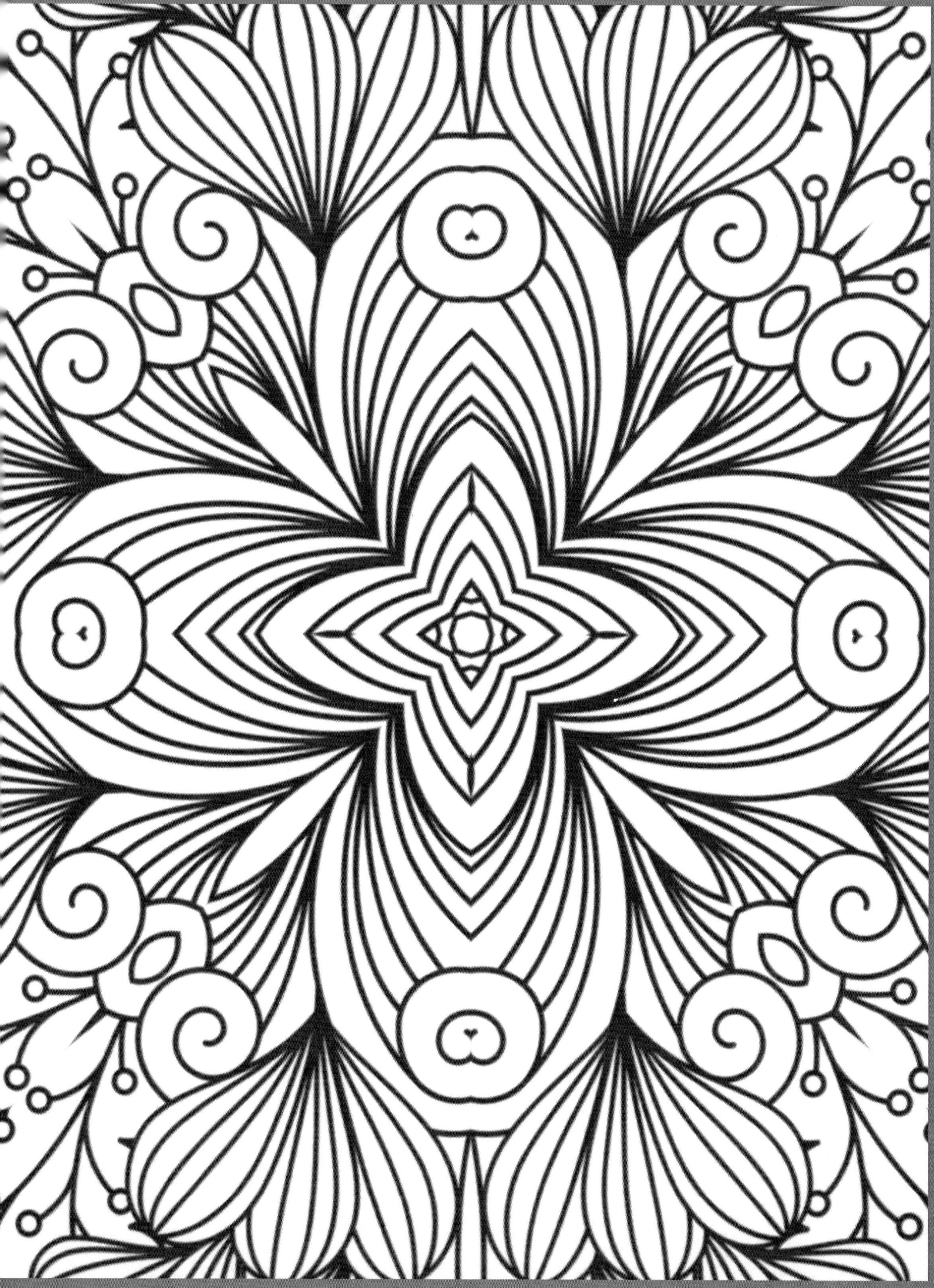

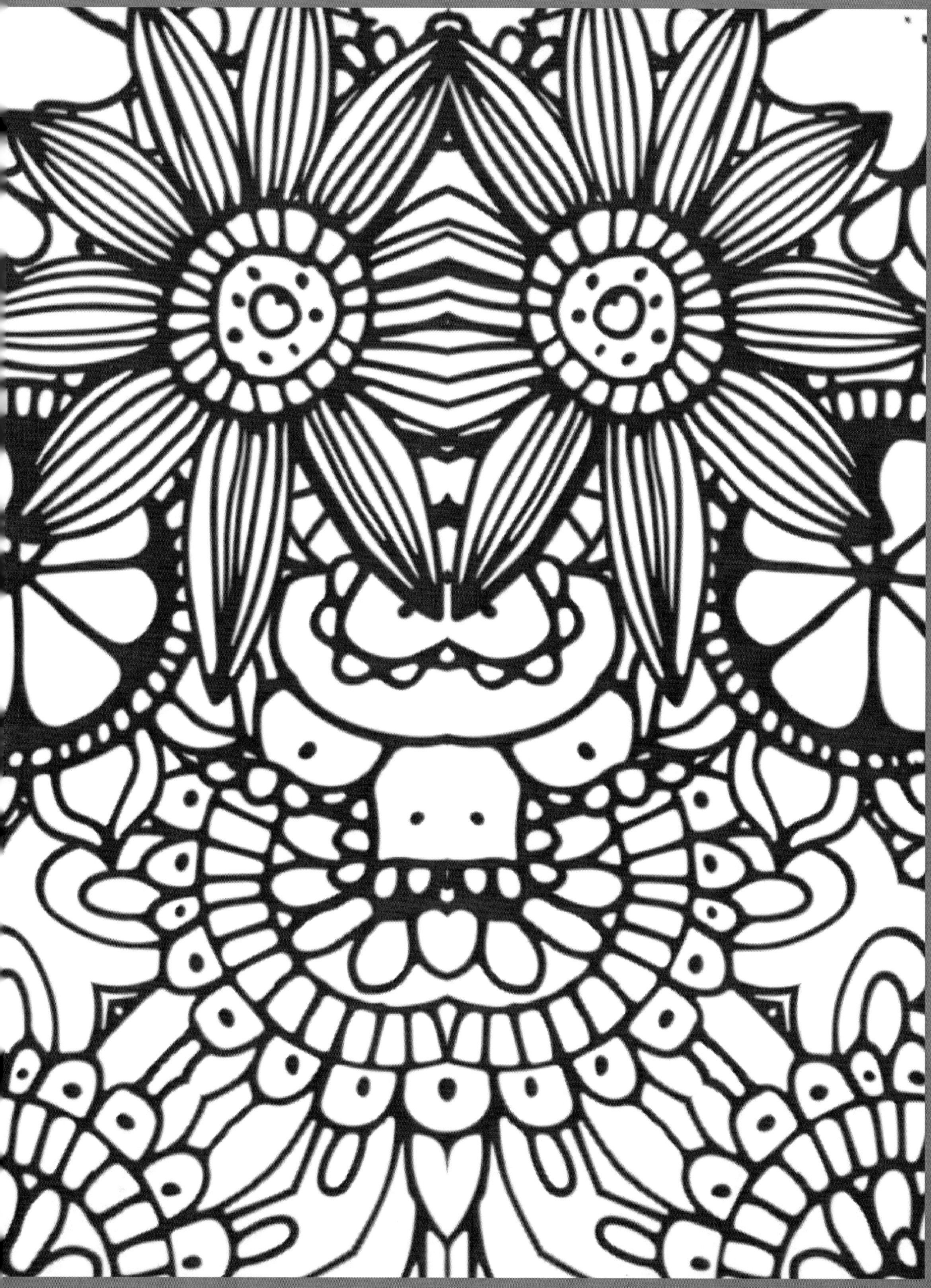

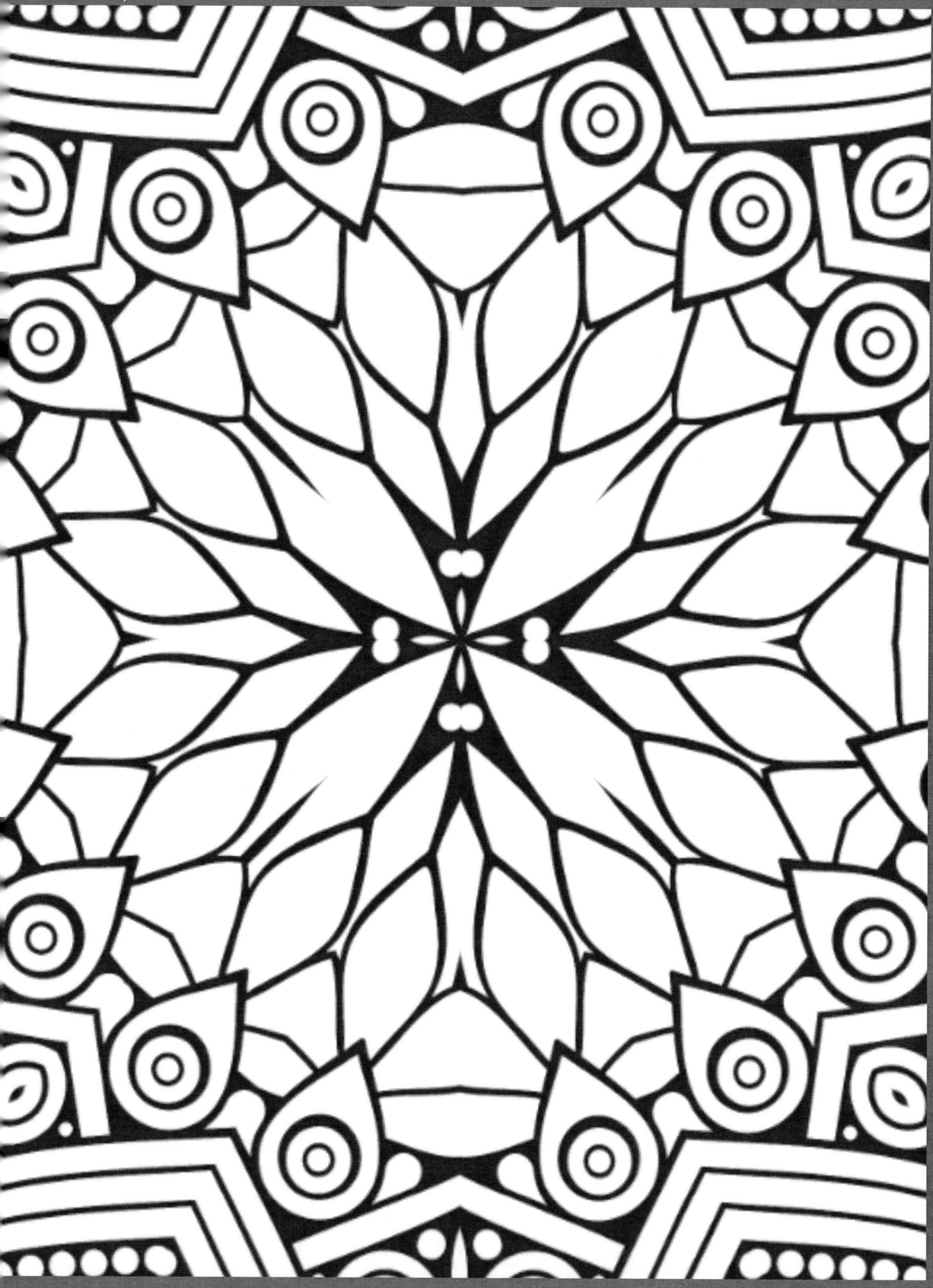

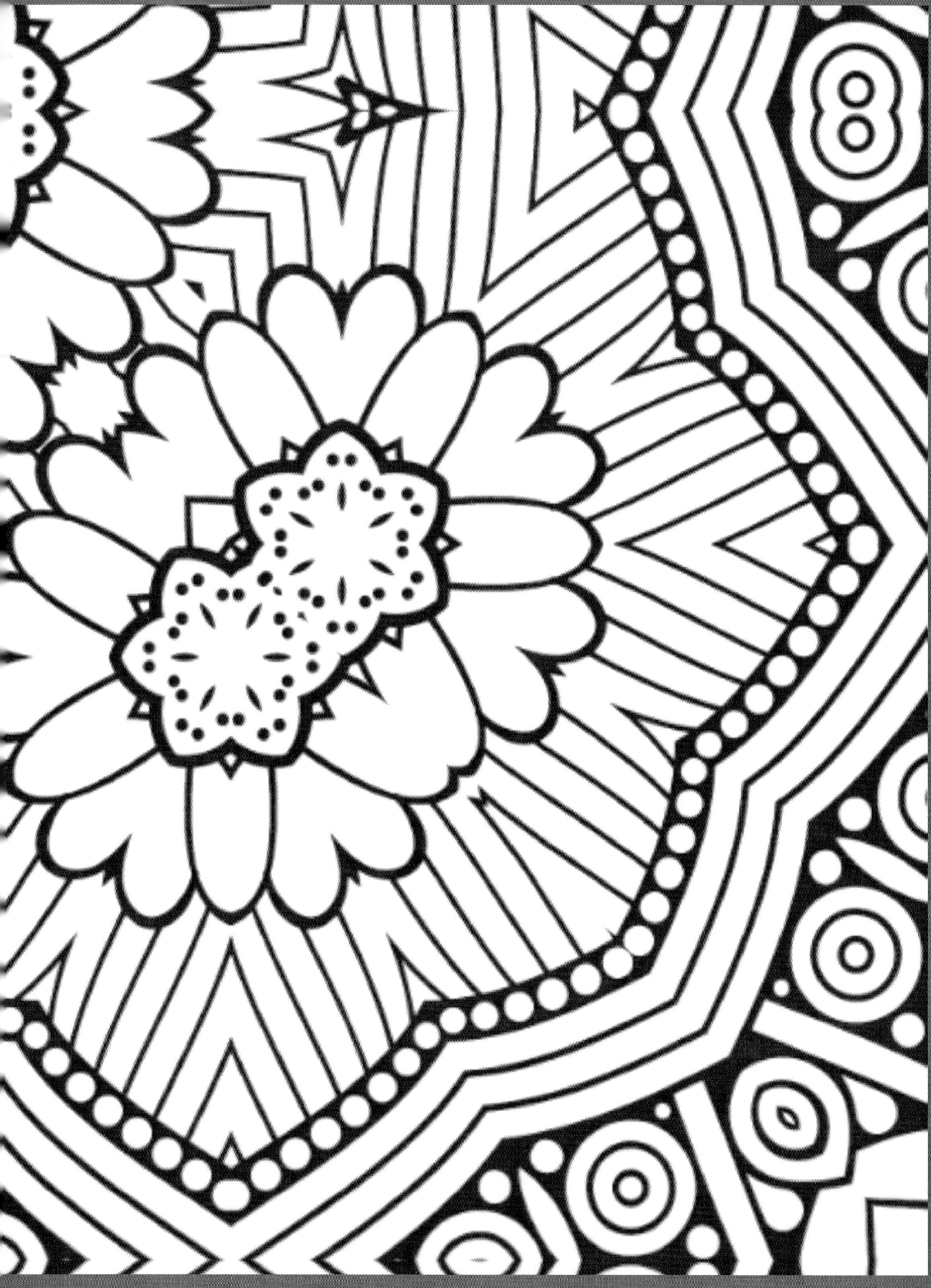

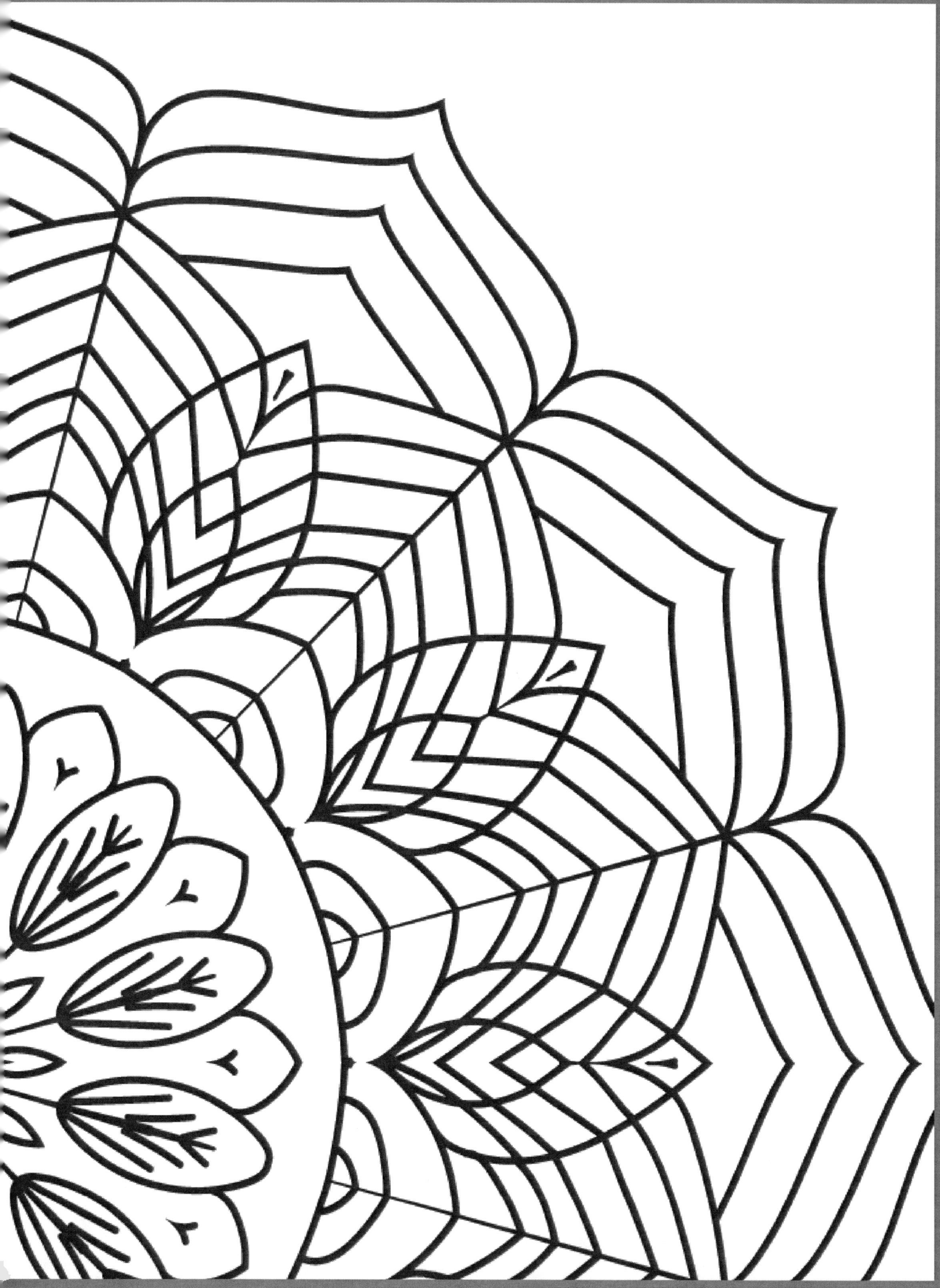

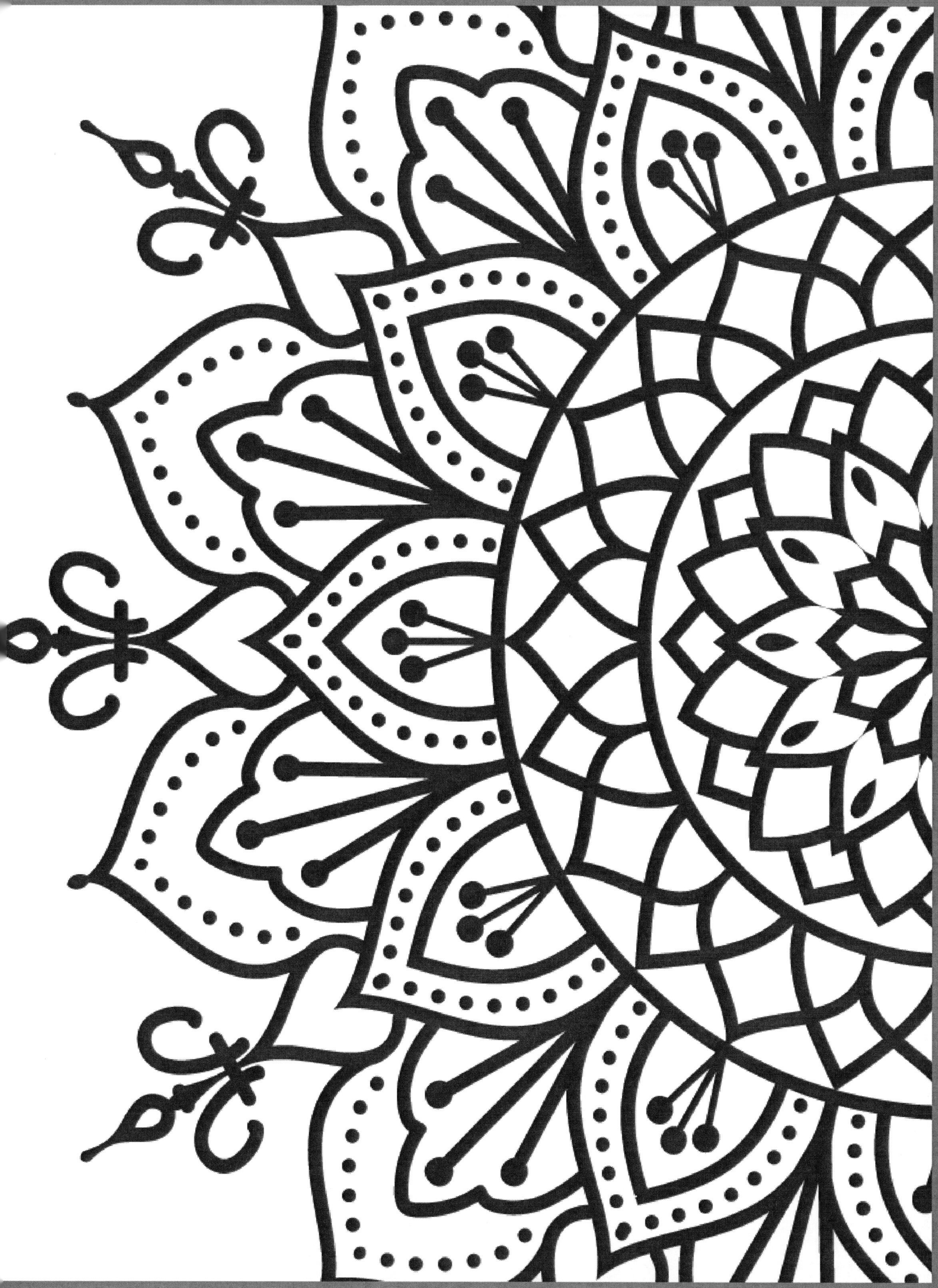

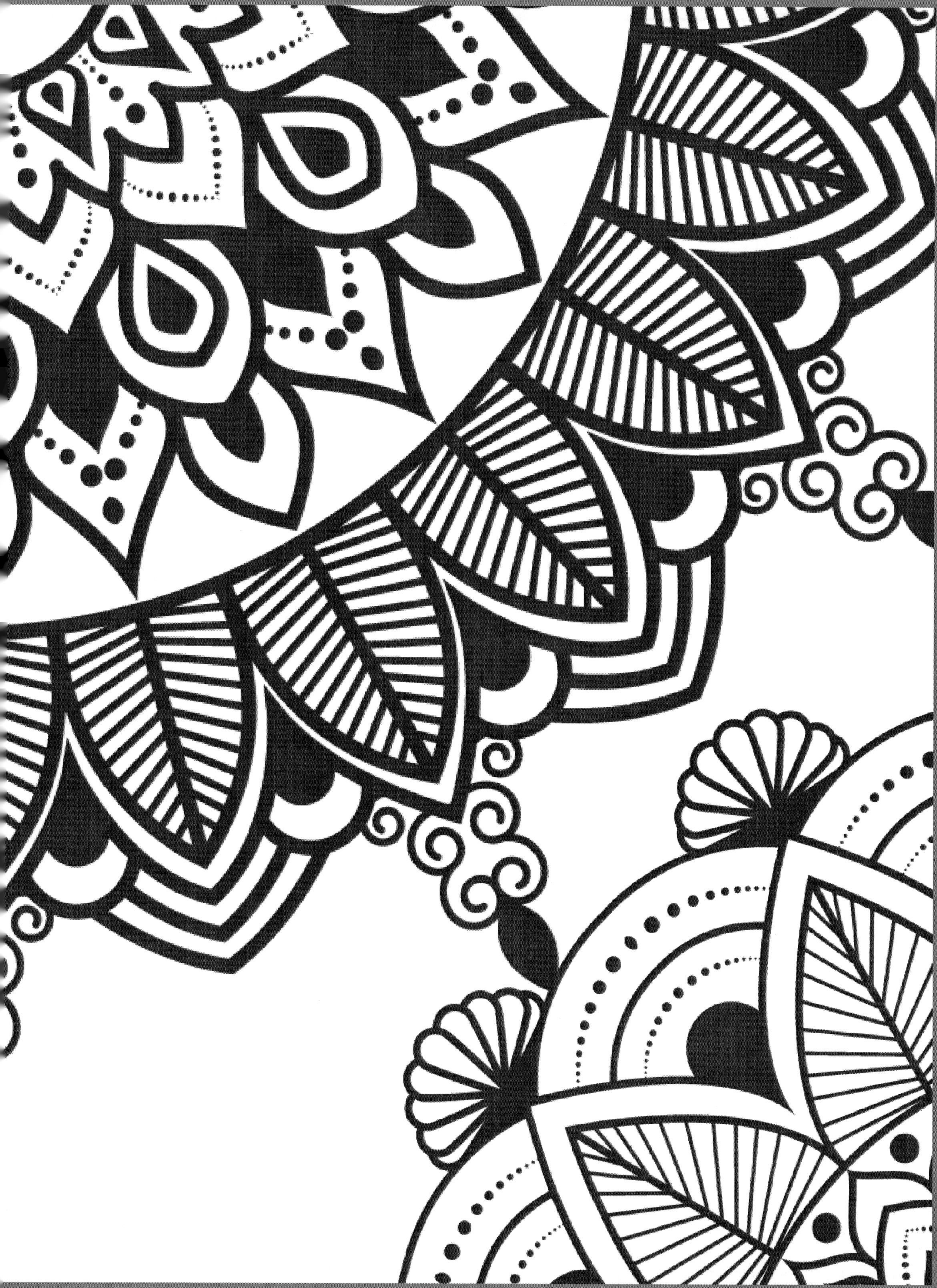

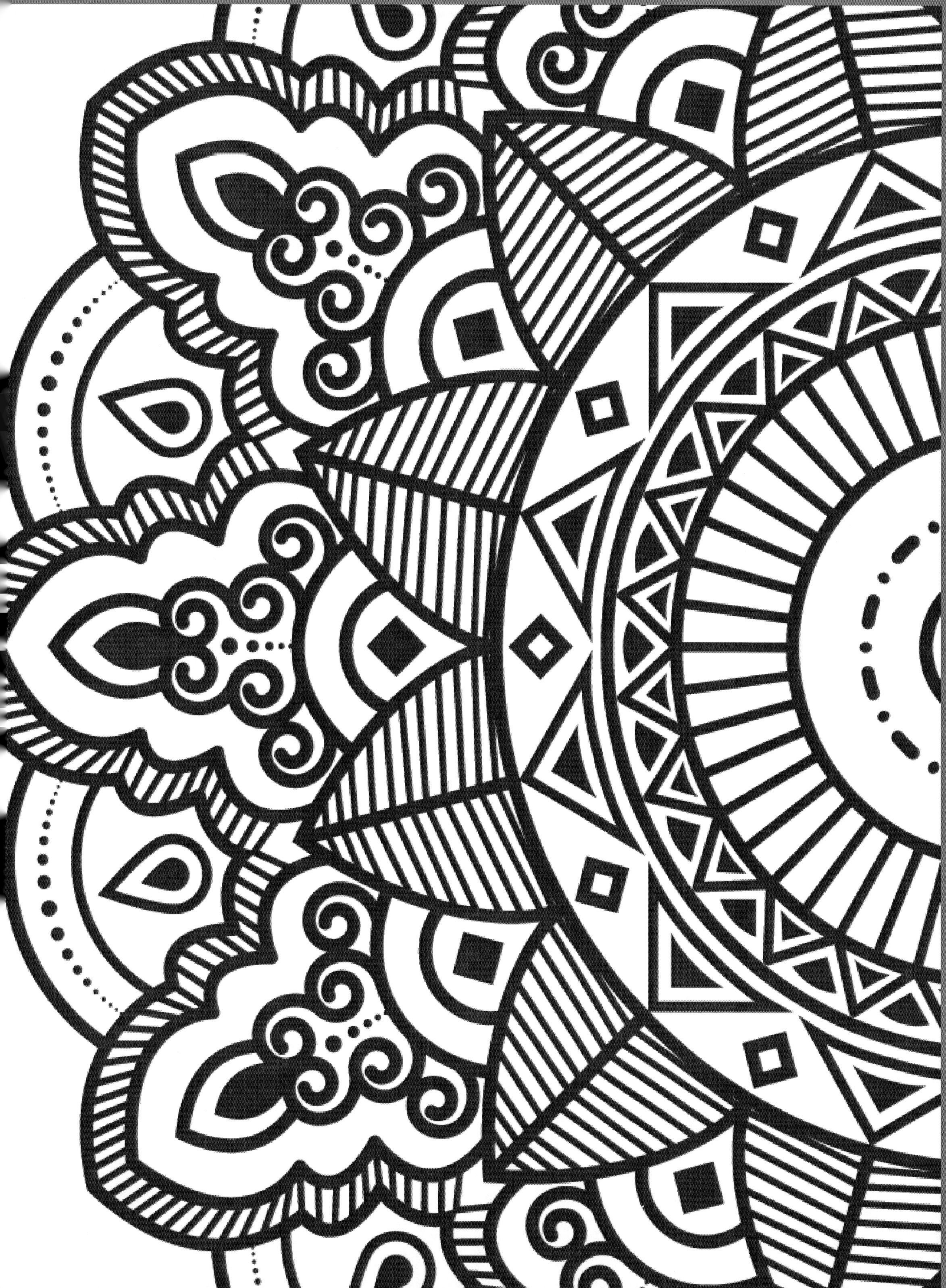

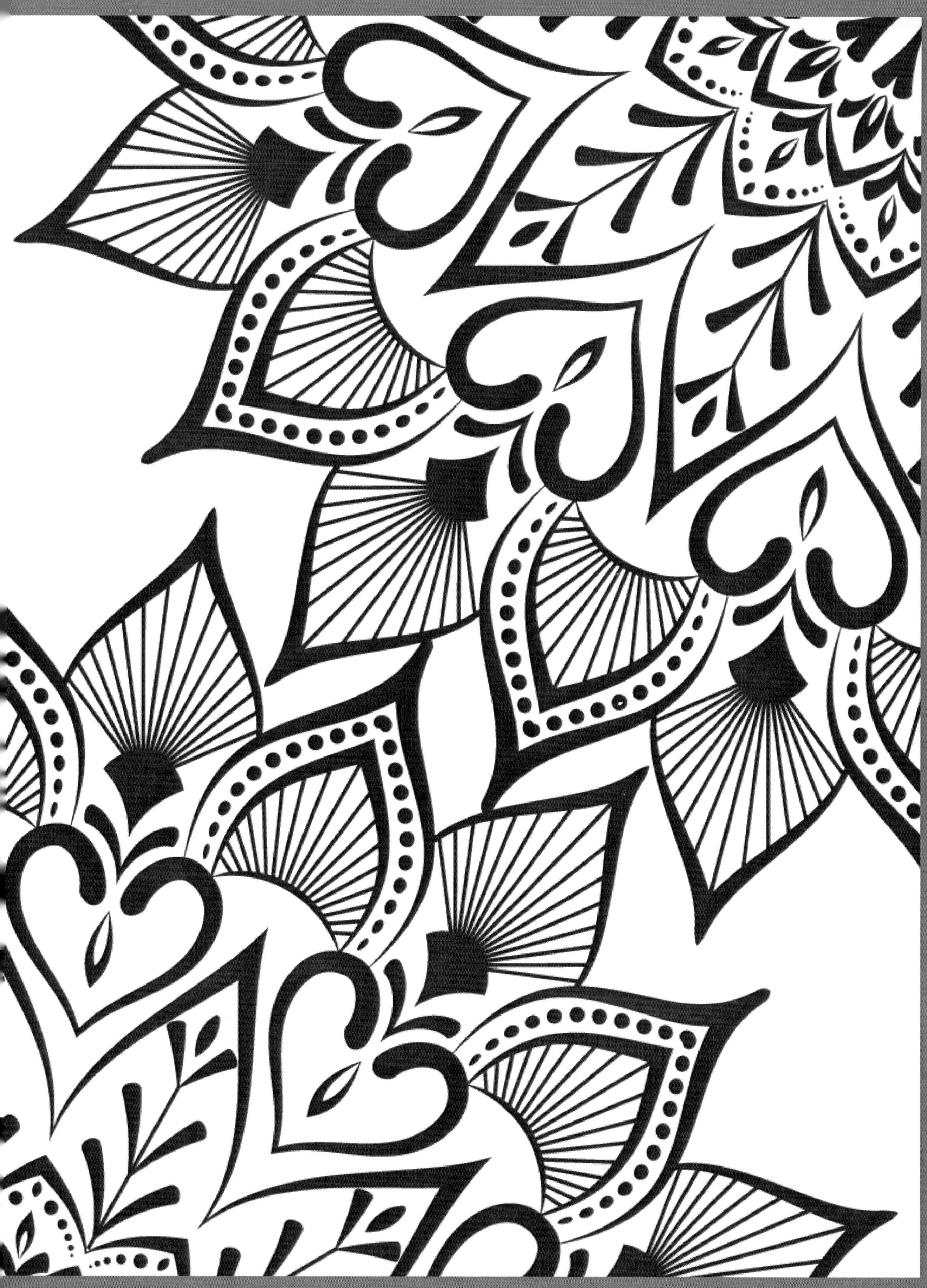

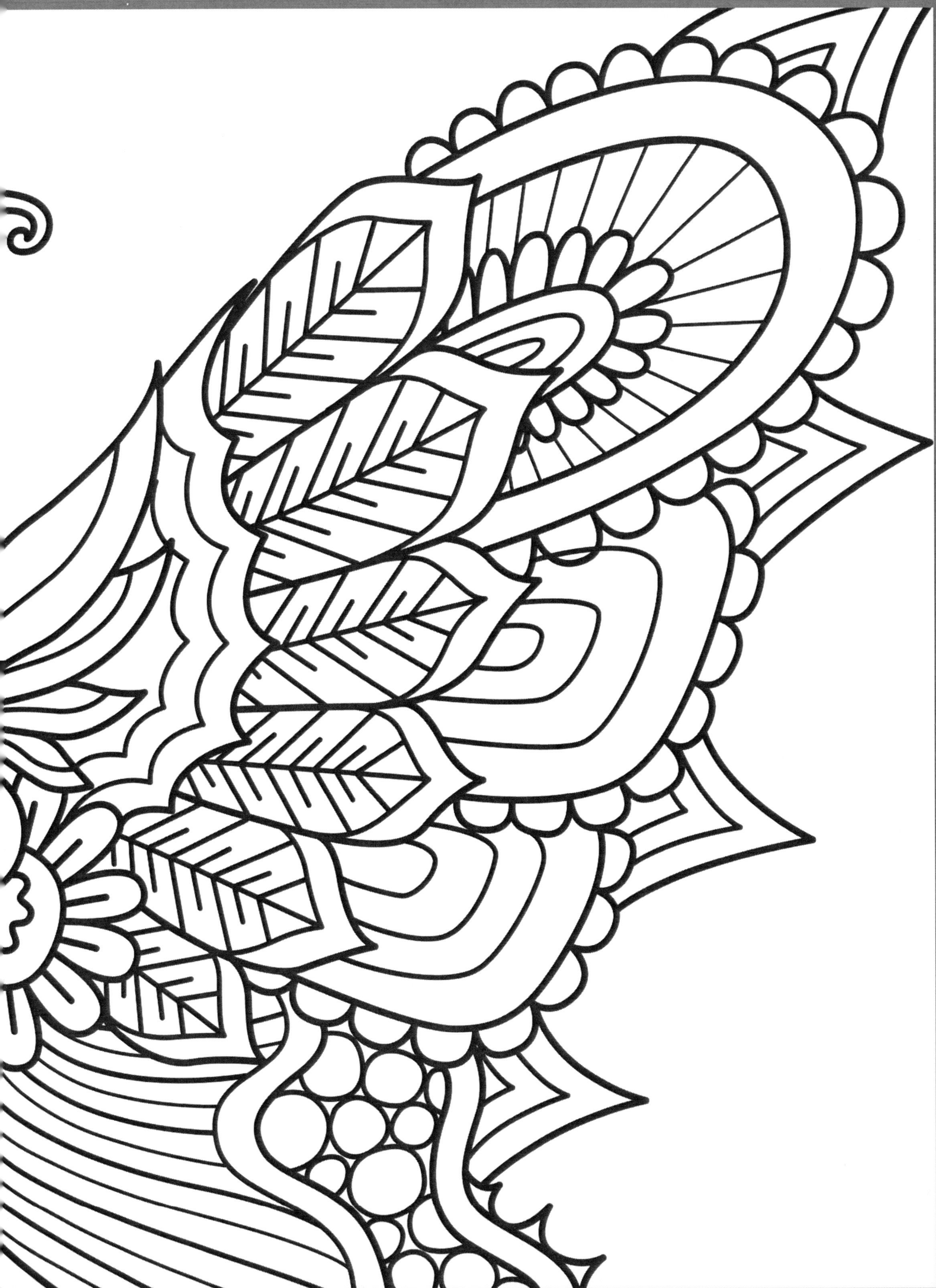

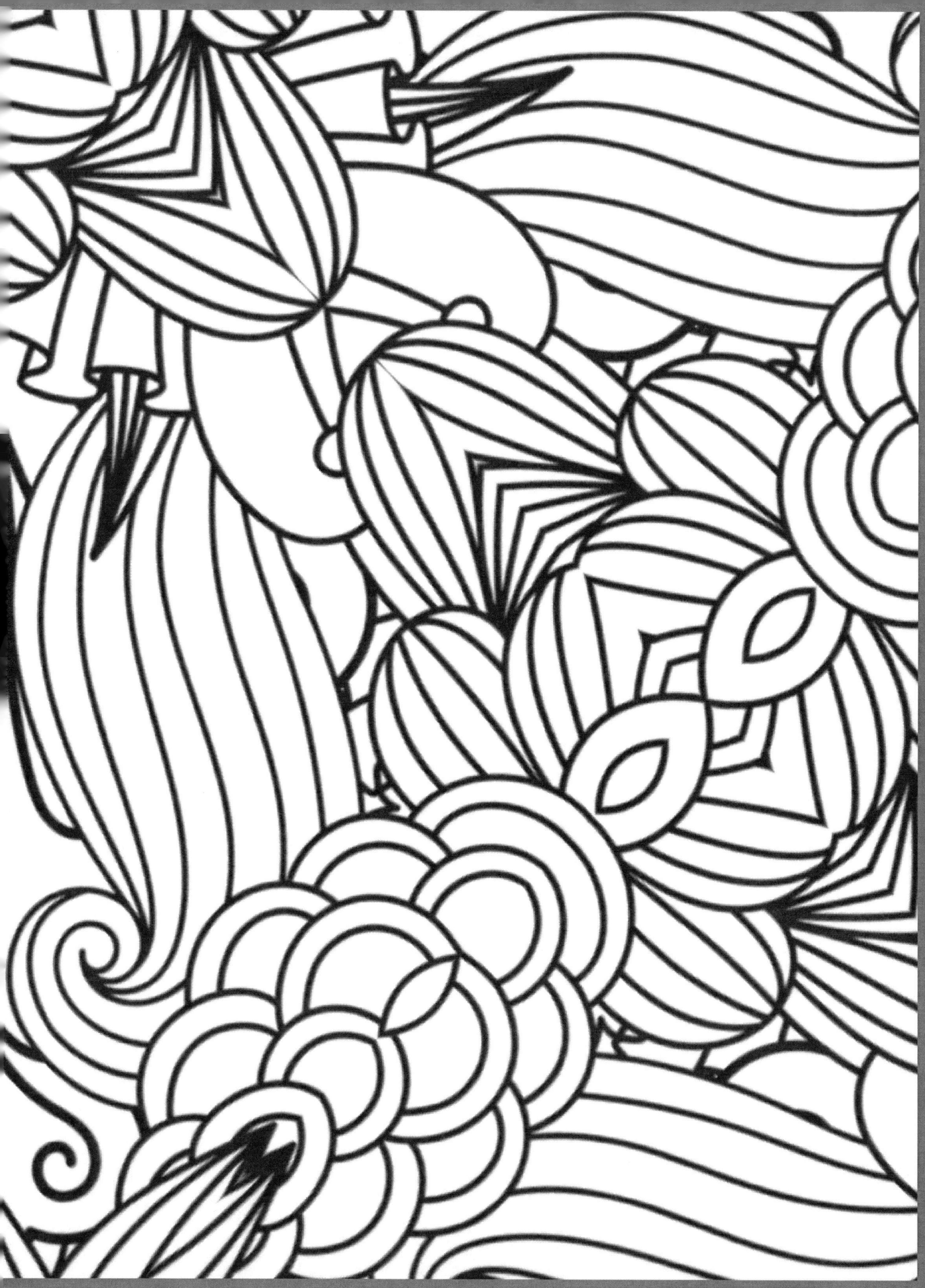

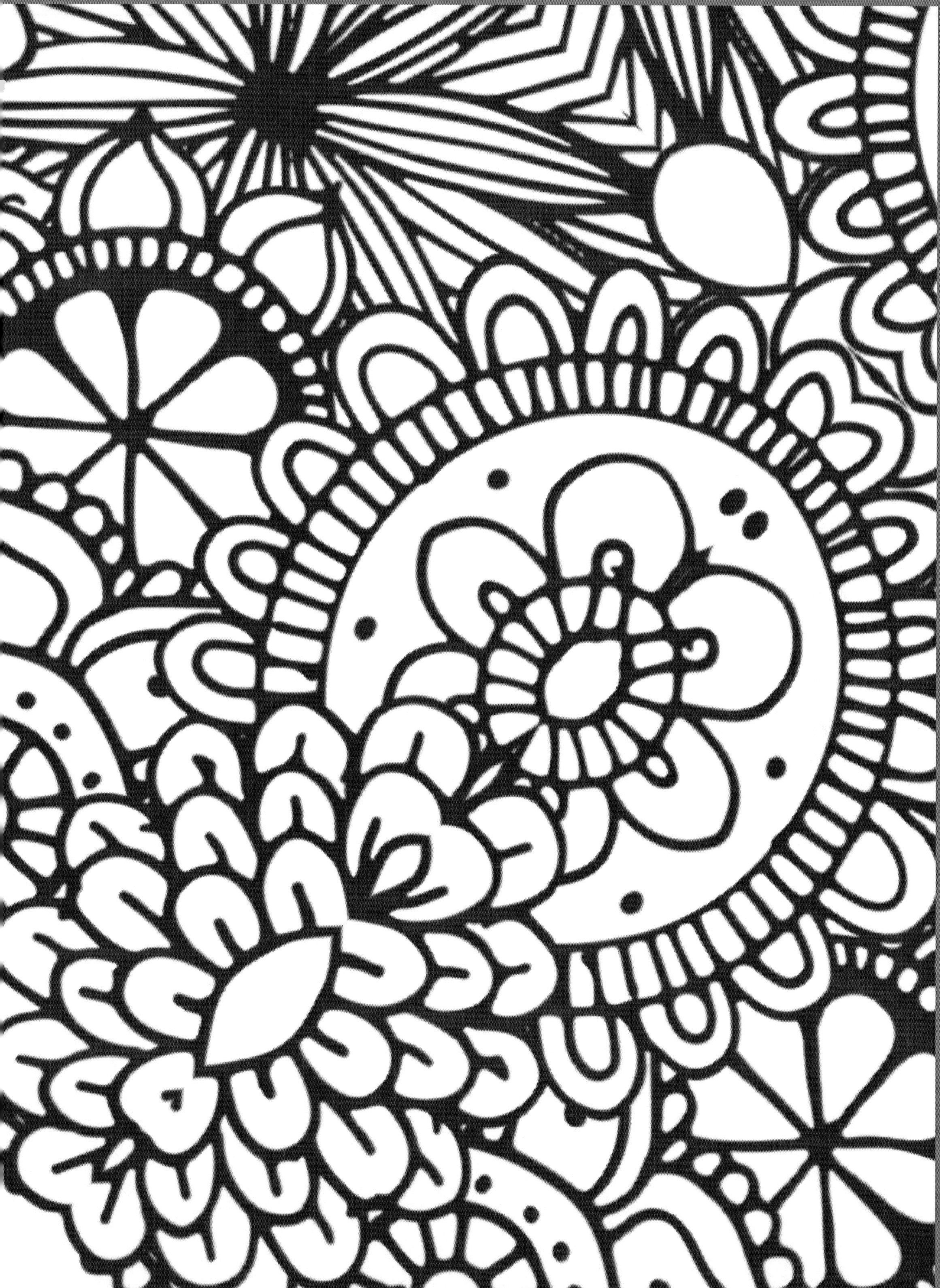

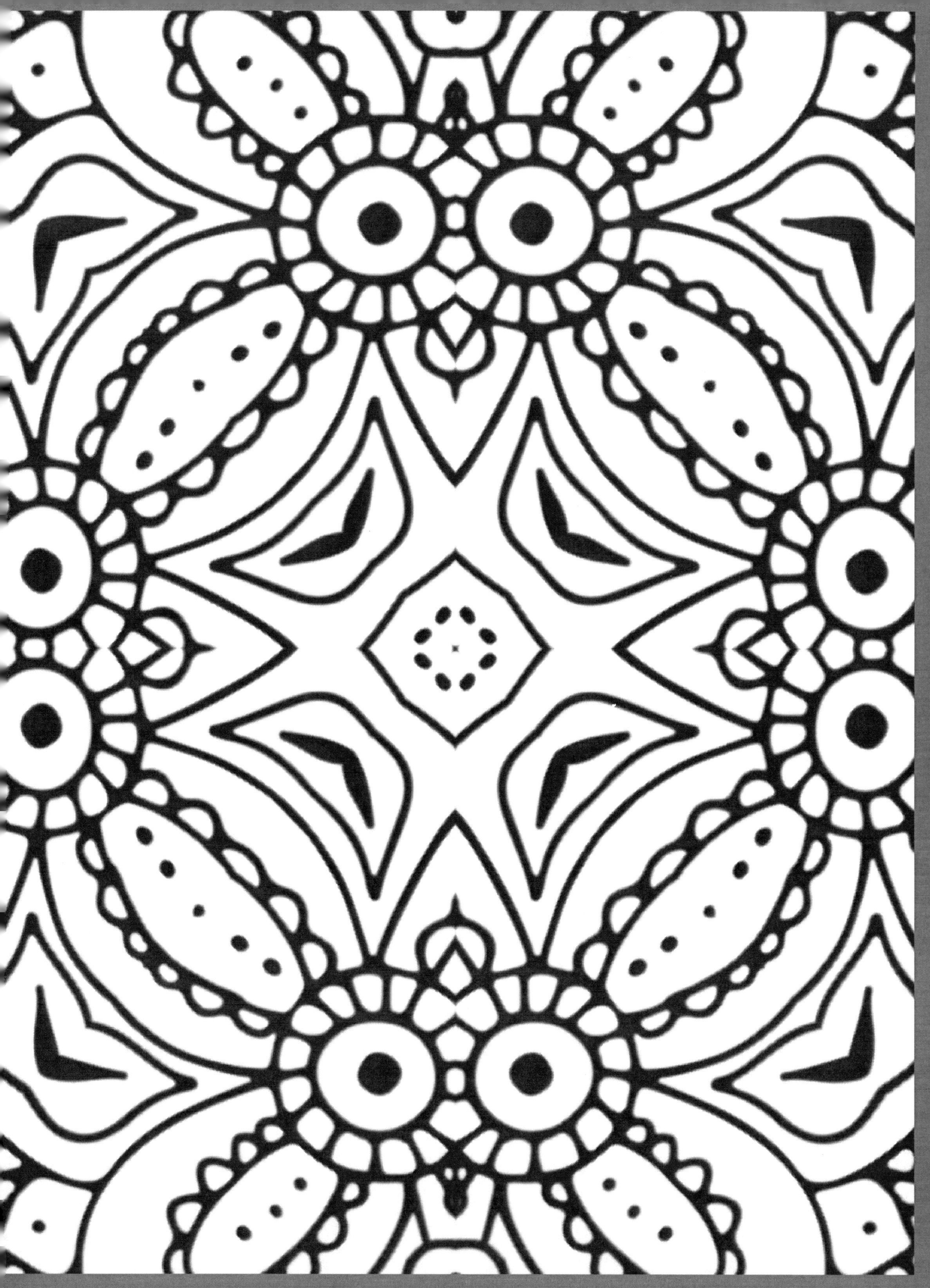

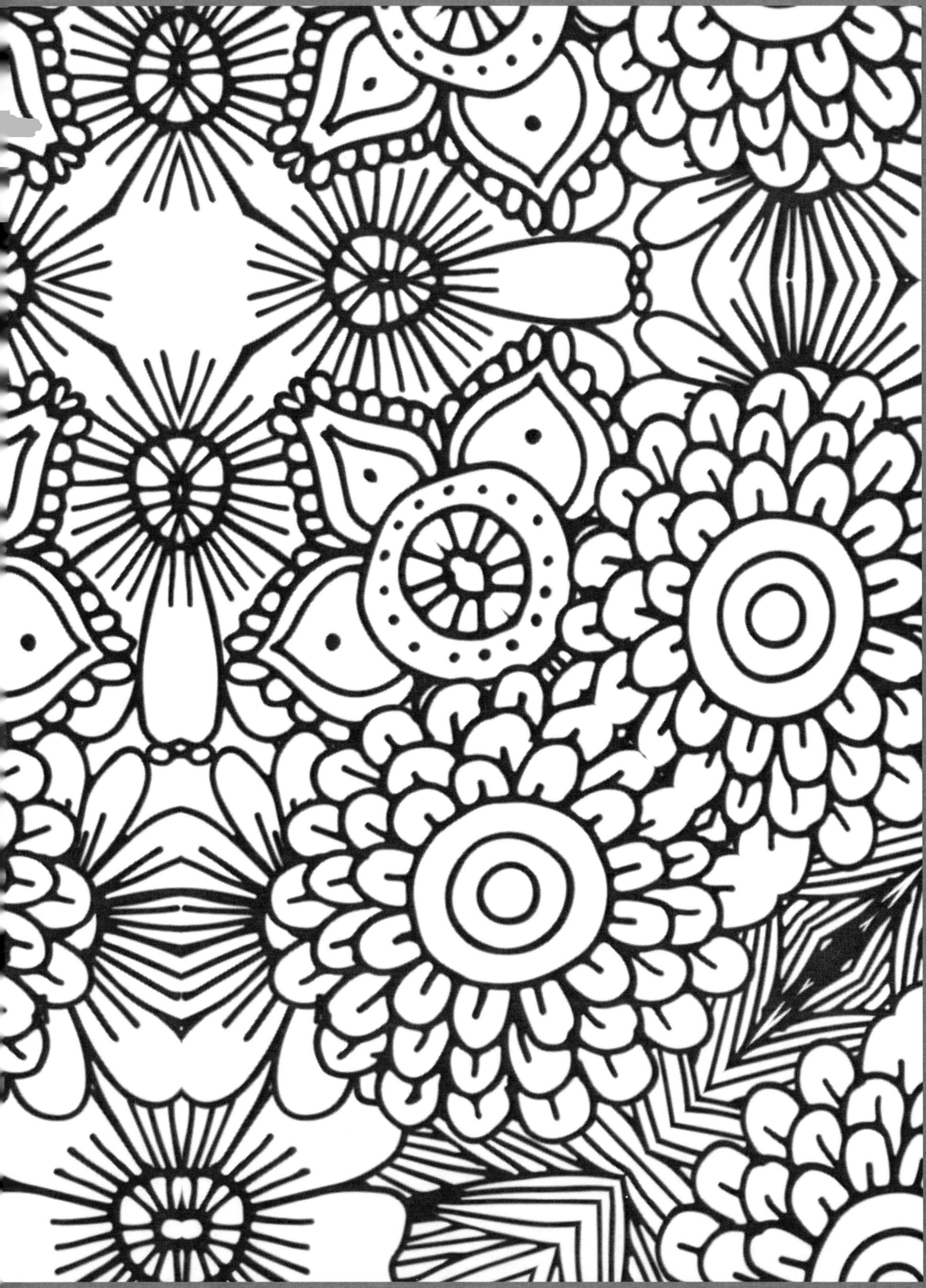

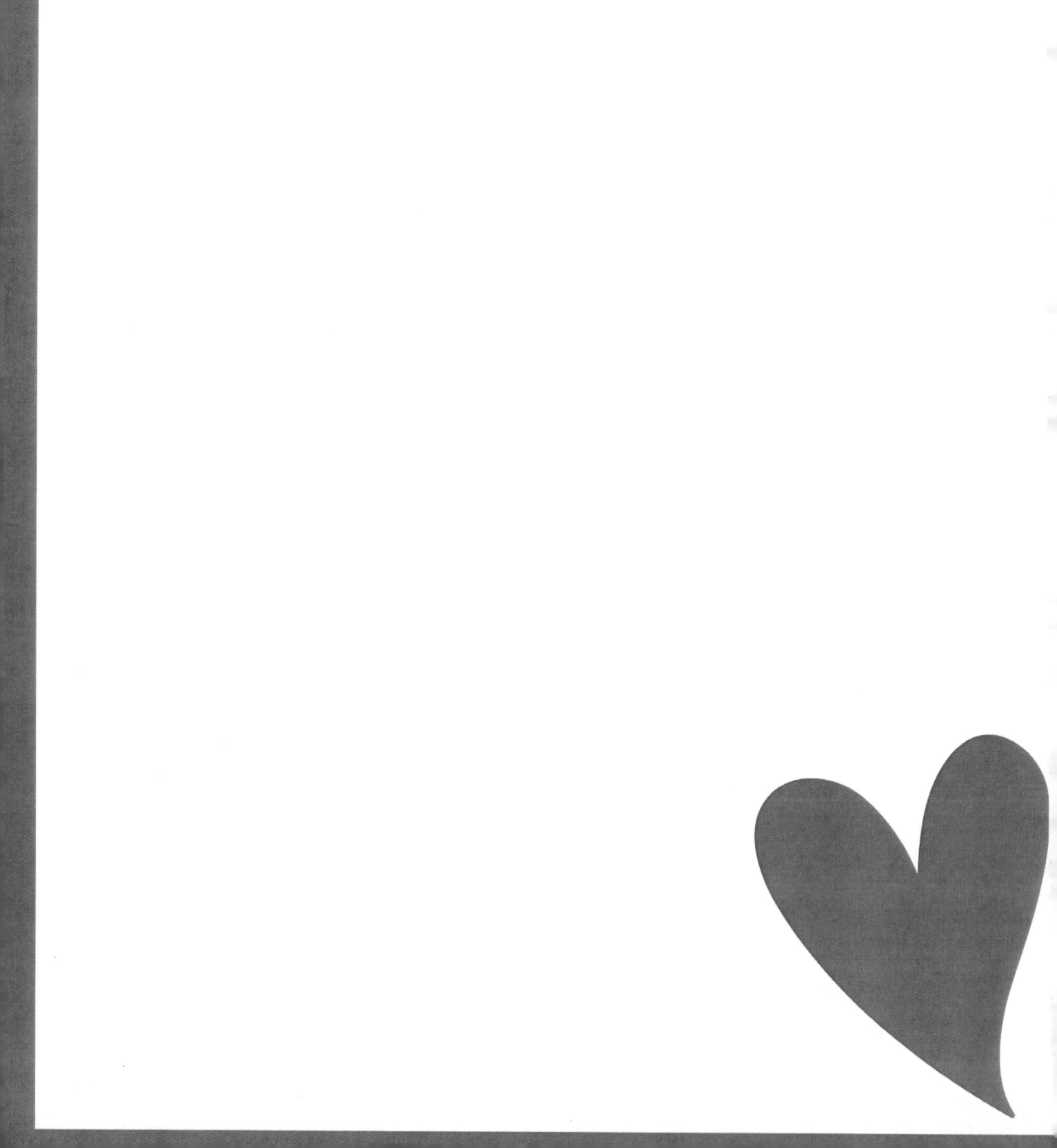

© Copyright 2023 - All rights reserved.

You may not be able to reproduce, duplicate or send the contents of this book without direct written permission from the author. You cannot with this despite any circumstance blame the publisher or hold him or her to legal responsibility for any reparation, compensation, or monetary forfeiture owing to the information included herein, either in a direct or an indirect way.

Legal Notice: This book has copyright protection. You can use the book for personal purposes. You should not sell, use, alter, distribute, quote, take excerpts, or paraphrase in part or whole the material contained in this book without obtaining the author's permission first.

Disclaimer Notice: You must take note that the information in this document is for casual reading and entertainment purposes only.

We have made every attempt to provide accurate, up-to-date, and reliable information. We do not express or implied guarantees of any kind. The persons who read admit that the writer is not occupied with giving legal, financial, medical, or other advice. We put this book content by sourcing various places.

Please consult a licensed professional before you try any techniques shown in this book. By going through this document, the book lover comes to an agreement that under no situation is the author accountable for any forfeiture, direct or indirect, which they may incur because of the use of material contained in this document, including, but not limited to, — errors, omissions, or inaccuracies.

Test your color here

Thank you!

We hope you enjoyed our book!

As a small family company, your feedback is very important to us to improve our work.

Please let us know how you like our book at:

ellafeedbackbooks@gmail.com

You can discover more books create by me on my author page.

Manufactured by Amazon.ca
Acheson, AB